THE CROSS

THE CROSS

God's Way of Salvation

D. MARTYN LLOYD-JONES

Edited by Christopher Catherwood

KINGSWAY PUBLICATIONS
EASTBOURNE

ISBN 0 86065 407 9

Unless otherwise indicated biblical quotations are from the
Authorized Version (crown copyright)
RV = Revised Version

Produced by Bookprint Creative Services
P.O. Box 827, BN21 3YJ, England for
KINGSWAY PUBLICATIONS LTD
Lottbridge Drove, Eastbourne, E Sussex BN23 6NT.
Printed in Great Britain

Contents

Foreword

There is little doubt that Dr Martyn Lloyd-Jones was the greatest preacher the Er.glish speaking world has seen in the twentieth century. Those of us who have had the privilege of hearing him will not easily forget the sense of awe which came upon one's soul as he was gripped by the glory of the gospel, and God spoke with such power through him. Yet it was not the man who lingered in the mind, nor was the lasting impression one of human gifts or intellectual ability, or personal magnetism. Rather, it was the power of truth, the greatness of God, the poverty of man, and the glorious relevance and authority of Holy Scripture which left an indelible mark on his hearers.

The publishing of his sermons must therefore be a cause of great gratitude throughout the Christian church. This particular series was preached in Westminster Chapel, London, in the autumn of 1963, all of them on the words of the Apostle in Galatians 6:14, 'God forbid that I should glory, save in the cross of our Lord Jesus Christ, by whom the world is crucified unto me and I unto the world.' They are a magnificent example of the Doctor's in-depth exposition of such a text, but they are also shining examples of his preaching Christ crucified.

Dr Lloyd-Jones' preaching was a remarkable combination of passionate eloquence and logical reasoning, of a profundity on which the maturest hearer had to ponder, with a simplicity that enabled even children to understand him. These characteristics are all illustrated in this series of sermons.

The need for them today could scarcely be greater, partly because of the decline in powerful biblical preaching in the English-speaking world, partly because of the theme. We urgently need to be recalled to this central truth of the Christian gospel, to explore it and proclaim it, and above all to glory in it. In another connection, Dr Lloyd-Jones once said, 'Superficial views of the work of Christ produce superficial Christian lives.'

May God abundantly use the reading of these pages to stimulate us to a new glorying in the cross, to a new desire for biblical preaching, and to a new love for Christ.

ERIC J. ALEXANDER
St George's, Tron, Glasgow

Introduction

Can you remember what you were doing when you heard the news that President Kennedy had been assassinated? Such was the shock of that event that it is said that people remember exactly where they were when they heard it. Even though I was only eight years old at the time, I can distinctly recall seeing the newsflash on the television announcing the tragedy that the President had been shot.

Another person who was shocked and saddened by Kennedy's tragic early death was Martyn Lloyd-Jones. It was the fact that the President was so young—cut down in the prime of life when his future seemed to promise so much—that perhaps struck people the most. Yet to Dr Lloyd-Jones, another death was far more important, and infinitely more relevant to the needs of the world in a strife-torn age. The death that really mattered was that of Jesus Christ on the cross at Calvary all those many years before.

Furthermore, unlike the death of President Kennedy, Christ's death on the cross was no tragedy but a glorious event. Indeed, the text on which this series of sermons is based, makes precisely this point. As Paul writes to the Galatians, 'But God forbid that I should glory, save in the cross of our Lord Jesus Christ.' To the Doctor, this was central.

Only in Jesus Christ was there any hope for today's world. Whereas the death of a mere man could cause despair, that of Jesus Christ gave life.

Sermons on the cross are normally associated with Easter, but these were preached at Westminster Chapel in the autumn of 1963. Towards the end of the series came the terrible news from Dallas of President Kennedy's assassination. The sermon delivered after the event shows what made the Doctor the particularly powerful preacher that he was. He did not, as some would have done today, interrupt his series to give a special address on the topic of John Kennedy's life. He continued with the series on Galatians that he had begun. Nor, on the other hand, did he ignore the event altogether, as many would have done. Instead he incorporated Kennedy's death into his sermon on Galatians.

For, to the Doctor, the cross had relevance to everything in life. Many had hoped that President Kennedy would bring peace to a world threatened by the prospect of nuclear holocaust—a threat that still very much hangs over us today. But, as Dr Lloyd-Jones points out, it is only Jesus Christ who can bring peace in the truest sense. God is sovereign and it is he, and not any human being, who decides the fate of the world.

Kennedy also did much to try to reconcile black and white Americans. But once again, the Doctor demonstrates that it is in the church of Jesus Christ, in those who have been redeemed by the blood of Calvary, that real multiracial unity is to be found.

It is not that the Doctor saw politics or social action by Christians as irrelevant or mistaken. He was fascinated by the political process all his life, ever since, as an adolescent, he sat in the gallery of the House of Commons watching Winston Churchill and David Lloyd-George engage in debate. He was all in favour of individual Christians becoming involved in politics, business, the arts and similar careers, and encouraged many to do so. It is rather that he understood from Scripture that the *ultimate* answer to man's problems lies not in man, but in Jesus Christ. This is the complete antithesis of Kennedy's own words at his inauguration when, quoting an Italian renaissance philosopher, he said that as man has created all his problems, so too can he solve them—to use the renaissance phrase, 'Man is the measure of all things, he can do all things if he will.' In the Doctor's view, the history of the twentieth century had shown beyond a doubt the sheer folly and bankruptcy of such a view.

Indeed, as these sermons show, the cross of Jesus Christ is as relevant today as it has ever been. It speaks to capitalists and communists alike, to all races, to every human being alive. Furthermore, as the Doctor makes clear, it is not enough merely for us to listen. For the message of the cross changes lives and demands a response from all who hear it. It is God's message of hope for today—there is no other.

CHRISTOPHER CATHERWOOD

But God forbid that I should glory, save in the cross of our Lord Jesus Christ, by whom the world is crucified unto me, and I unto the world.

Galatians 6:14

During these twenty-six years in my Westminster pulpit there have been times when in my utter folly I have wondered, or the Devil has suggested to me that there is nothing more for me to say, that I have preached it all. I thank God that I can now say that I feel I am only at the beginning of it. There is no end to this glorious message of the cross, for there is always something new and fresh and entrancing and moving and uplifting that one has never seen before.

Martyn Lloyd-Jones

Chapter 1

'The Wondrous Cross'

Give me the faith which can remove
    And sink the mountain to a plain;
Give me the childlike, praying love
    Which longs to build Thy house again;
Thy love, let it my heart o'erpower,
Let it my ransomed soul devour.

I would the precious time redeem
    And longer live for this alone—
To spend and to be spent for them
    Who have not yet my Saviour known;
Fully on these my mission prove,
And only breathe, to breathe Thy love.

My talents, gifts and graces, Lord,
    Into Thy blessed hands receive;
And let me live to preach Thy word,
    And let me to Thy glory live;
My every sacred moment spend
In publishing the sinners' Friend.

Enlarge, inflame and fill my heart
    With boundless charity divine;
So shall I all my strength exert,
    And love them with a zeal like Thine;
And lead them to Thine open side,
The sheep for whom their shepherd died.

C. Wesley

Could you and would you gladly spend all your days in that way? That is the question. Is it your desire to spend all your days in praising this friend, of whom all those words are true?

Well, in order to try to help you to answer that question, I would like to call your attention to the words found in Paul's epistle to the Galatians. In chapter 6 verse 14, he writes: 'But God forbid that I should glory, save in the cross of our Lord Jesus Christ, by whom the world is crucified unto me, and I unto the world.' Now, this verse follows on from what went before, the word 'but' suggests it. Verses 12 and 13 read like this: 'As many as desire to make a fair shew in the flesh, they constrain you to be circumcised; only lest they should suffer persecution for the cross of Christ. For neither they themselves who are circumcised keep the law; but desire to have you circumcised, that they may glory in your flesh. But God forbid that I should glory, save in the cross of our Lord Jesus Christ, by whom the world is crucified unto me, and I unto the world.'

As I have just reminded you, this statement can only be understood properly if we also take it in its own context, since this helps us to see why the Apostle speaks as he does in this way about the death of the Son of God, our Lord and Saviour, Jesus Christ, upon the cross on Calvary's hill. He is finishing his letter to the Galatians. These were people who had become Christians as the result of his own preaching and teaching. But certain other teachers had gone round, who had been upsetting them. They had taught that while it is all right to believe in the gospel, yet, if you really want to be a full blown Christian and want to be truly blessed of God, you have also got to submit to circumcision and go back under the old Jewish law. The Apostle has written this, his own epistle, in order to deal with that question. And here he is now at the very end of his letter summarizing all he has been saying. And, at the same time, he is reminding the Galatians, and all others through them, of certain fundamental truths and principles of the Christian faith.

The first thing of which he reminds them is that life in this world is a very serious and a very solemn matter. Life when truly understood is not the sort of thing that the world would teach you to think of, it is not something flippant and light, through which you waltz having a good time. Not at all. It is a tremendously serious matter. For this reason: 'Be not deceived; God is not mocked: for whatsoever a man soweth, that shall he also reap. For he that soweth to his flesh shall of the flesh reap corruption; but he that soweth to the Spirit shall of the Spirit reap life everlasting' (vv.7–8).

Life is a matter of sowing and reaping, and what a man sows that shall he also reap. There are certain moral laws in operation in this world which are absolute. All of us are responsible beings, and we shall all die and stand before God in judgement and give account of the deeds done in the body. And our eternal destiny will depend upon what we have done in this life and in this world. Life therefore is a tremendous matter. It is the most serious thing conceivable, because what we get in this life and what we will get through all eternity depends upon whether we sow to the flesh or whether we sow to the Spirit.

Very well then, the most important thing to discover in this world is—how does one sow to the Spirit? How am I so to live that I shall reap the blessing of joy and happiness and peace in this world and in the world to come for ever and for ever? That is the question, but unfortunately, as the Apostle goes on to point out, and as indeed he has been indicating in the whole of his epistle, that question, that problem, has become somewhat confused, because there are false teachers. The position had arisen in the early church, and it still remains today. There are contradictory voices going out in the name of the Christian church. They all say they are Christians, all claim to belong to the Christian church, but they are saying things that are diametrically opposed to one another. So the first thing we have to do is to discover which is the true message. How do you differentiate between the true and the false? The Apostle has answered the question in this epistle, as he has answered it in other epistles. As indeed the whole of the Bible answers it.

What then is the true message? What is the Christian gospel? What is it about? What does it proclaim? What has it got to say to us? How can a man be right with God? How can I sow to the Spirit? How can I reap life everlasting? What have I got to do in this life and in this world which will render me immune to what may happen round and about me, which would enable me to smile in the face of death, which already assures me that I have nothing to fear when I come to the judgement of God, and which guarantees me everlasting and eternal bliss in the glory indescribable? What have I got to do? How can I get to that position? Here, very fortunately for us, the great apostle answers the question. He puts it in this glorious and tremendous statement. 'God forbid that I should glory ...' the thing is unthinkable, he says, that I should glory in anything '... save in the cross of our Lord Jesus Christ, by whom the world is crucified unto me and I unto the world.' This is the thing in which he glories. This is the thing which he preached. And this by the grace of God is the thing that I am privileged to preach to you. It is the same answer, there is still only this one message.

What is it? Let us look at it like this. The preaching of the cross, the preaching of the death of the Lord Jesus Christ on that cross is the very heart and centre of the Christian gospel and the Christian message. Now, I think you must all agree that that is an inevitable deduction, both from what the Apostle says here and from what he picks out as that in

which he glories. The central thing, the thing that matters
above everything else, and what he picks out is the cross,
the death on the cross of our Lord Jesus Christ.

This is, as I want to show you, what he always preached,
and what all the other apostles always preached. If you and I
want to know what the message of the Christian church is,
surely the thing for us to do is to go back to the beginning.
How did the Christian church begin? What was the message?
Here are men called apostles. These were the men who
founded the Christian church. They all said that they were
not preaching their own ideas, but that they had been given
the message by the Lord Jesus Christ. So, if we want to know
what the Christian message is we must go back and consider
the Apostle's message. And that is what we are going to do
now. And I hope to show you that the message was the cross
of our Lord Jesus Christ.

Now, what I want to emphasize is that this is what they
preached, and that they did so in spite of the fact that it was
not popular. The preaching of the cross has never been
popular. It is not popular today. It never has been. The
preaching of the cross was a stumbling block to the Jews, it
was foolishness to the Greeks. Paul says, 'As many as desire
to make a fair show in the flesh, they constrain you to be
circumcised' (v. 12). And this is their reason, 'lest they should
suffer persecution for the cross of Christ.' The preaching of
the cross of Christ has always led to persecution. Earlier in
the same epistle, the Apostle speaks about what he describes
as the offence of the cross. It has always been offensive to
people. They did not like it in the first century, the Jews did
not, the Greeks did not, nobody liked it. Nevertheless, in
spite of the fact that it was not liked and that it was thoroughly
unpopular, this was the very thing that all the apostles
preached. They went on preaching and eventually suffered
martyrdom and death because they persisted in doing so.

This then establishes the fact that it was the very centre and heart of their message, and there is nothing that I know of that is more important than that every one of us should realize that this is still the heart and the centre of the Christian message. In order to emphasize that, let me put it negatively first. What is the message of the Christian gospel, and of the Christian church? Now at the risk of being misunderstood I will put it like this. It is not primarily the *teaching* of our Lord. I say that, of course, because there are so many today who think that this is Christianity. They say: 'What we need is Jesus's teaching. He is the greatest religious genius of all times. He is above all the philosophers. Let us have a look at his teaching, at the Sermon on the Mount and so on. That is what we want. What the world needs today,' they say, 'is a dose of the Sermon on the Mount. A dose of his ethical teaching. We must preach this to people and teach them how to live.' But according to the apostle Paul, that is not their first need. And I will go further. If you only preach the teaching of the Lord Jesus Christ, not only do you not solve the problem of mankind, in a sense you even aggravate it. You are preaching nothing but utter condemnation, because nobody can ever carry it out.

So they did not preach his teaching. Paul does not say, 'God forbid that I should glory, save in the Sermon on the Mount; God forbid that I should glory save in the ethical teaching of Jesus.' He does not say that. It was not the teaching of Christ, nor the example of Christ either. That is often preached, is it not? 'What is the message of Christianity? The imitation of Christ. Read the Gospels,' they say, 'and see how he lived. That is the way we all ought to live, so let us decide to do so. Let us decide to imitate Christ and to live as he lived.'

I say once more that that is not the centre and the heart of the Christian message. That comes into it, but not at the beginning. It is not the first thing, it is not the thing the apostles preached initially, neither was it our Lord's example. What they preached was his death upon the cross, and the meaning of that event. Now this is an assertion, and of course I must substantiate it, because people are ready to say, 'Yes, but that is only your opinion. You have attacked the other opinions, and of course like all you preachers, you say that you alone are right.' But, my dear friends, I want to show· you that this is not *my* opinion. I am going to establish what I have said from the book called the New Testament, which is a book written by or derived from apostles and their apostolic authority.

What, then, do you find when you examine the book? You find that the cross was there at the centre of our Lord's own teaching. There is a very striking illustration of this that people do not often remember. It is the event that happened at Caesarea Philippi, and what immediately followed it. There, you remember, our Lord turned to his disciples and said, 'Whom do men say that I am?' and they gave various answers. And then he said, 'Whom say ye that I am?' and Peter stepped forward and said, 'Thou art the Christ, the. Son of the living God.' And our Lord turned to him and said, 'Blessed art thou, Simon Bar-jona: for flesh and blood hath not revealed it unto thee, but my Father which is in heaven.' And then he went on to say, 'Thou art Peter, upon this rock I will build my church' (Mt 16:13–18).

But then read on: 'From that time forth began Jesus to shew unto his disciples, how that he must go unto Jerusalem, and suffer many things of the elders and chief priests and scribes and be killed, and be raised again the third day. Then Peter took him and began to rebuke him, saying, Be it far from thee, Lord: this shall not be unto thee. But he turned, and said unto Peter, Get thee behind me, Satan: for thou art an offence unto me: for thou savourest not the things that be of God, but those that be of men' (Mt 16:21–23).

Now, you see after this great confession of Peter that Jesus is the Christ, the Son of the Living God, the Lord immediately introduces them to his death, and they cannot take it. Peter was not the only one who failed, they all did so. Our Lord rebukes him and tells him in effect, 'You do not understand. You think that the fact that I am the Son of God is the thing that is going to save you. It is not. It is what I am going to do.'

And then of course you have other statements. There is that great statement recorded in all the Gospels where the Lord turned to these same men and said, You have got to rethink the whole matter. I am a king. I have a kingdom, but it is not like the kingdom of men, nor is it like all the other kingdoms in this world. In this world great men are served by others. But I come amongst you as one who ministers. 'For the Son of man came not to be ministered unto, but to minister, and to give his life a ransom for many' (Mt 20:28).

And then there is the last supper. He arranged it. He told them exactly what to do. And there, as they were eating, he took the loaf and he broke it and he said, 'This is my body which is given for you' and likewise he poured out the wine from the cup and said, 'This cup is the new testament in my blood, which is shed for you' (Lk 22:19,20). This, he says, is my giving myself, my body to be broken, my blood to be shed for you. Well there it is, plainly and clearly and simply in his teaching. But then in addition we have other things which might pinpoint this. Do you remember the amazing event which took place on the Mount of Transfiguration? Our Lord went up on to a mountain taking Peter and James and John with him, and there he was transfigured before them, and two men, Moses and Elijah, appeared in spirit form and they spoke to him while the three disciples looked on in amazement. But what was the conversation about?

What did Moses and Elijah discuss with our Lord? We are told that they discussed with him the exit, the exodus, that he would be making outside the walls of Jerusalem. They discussed his death with him. The representatives of the law and of the Prophets discussed with him his death upon the cross. The cross is vital.

Not only that, we read of him later on that he set his face steadfastly to go to Jerusalem even though he knew exactly what was going to happen to him. And here is another notable fact if you are interested in statistics. Read your four Gospels and calculate, in terms of proportion, the amount of space given to our Lord's death. Though they are very brief records, look how much space is given to the account of the death. See how we are given every detail. In fact, as someone once pointed out, it is so graphic and so detailed, we could almost hear the sound of the hammer knocking the nails into his hands and into his feet.

Why this prominence? It is because it is the crucial and the central matter. There it is in the Gospels, and when you come to the book of Acts of the Apostles, what do you find? Read Acts 13:14–41 in order to make the matter absolutely clear. Paul, preaching to the people of Antioch, went over the facts with them, emphasizing especially the Lord's death and resurrection. Then he applied his message saying that through this man and through this event salvation is preached and is offered (v. 38). This is the wonderful thing. And then you go on further to chapter 17 and read about Paul visiting Thessalonica. This is what happened: 'Paul, as his manner was, went in unto them and three sabbath days reasoned with them out of the scriptures, opening and alleging, that Christ must needs have suffered, and risen again from the dead; and that this Jesus, whom I preach unto you, is Christ' (17:2–3). That indeed was his preaching everywhere, as it was the preaching of all the other apostles.

And then you come on to the epistles. I could, by just quoting scriptures to you, prove that this is the central message of the Christian gospel. There is a wonderful one, that I cannot refrain from quoting, in Romans 3: 'Therefore by the deeds of the Law there shall no flesh be justified in his sight: for by the law is the knowledge of sin. But now the righteousness of God without the law [apart from the law] is manifested, being witnessed by the law and the prophets; even the righteousness of God which is by faith of Jesus Christ unto all and upon all them that believe: for there is no difference: for all have sinned, and come short of the glory of God; being justified freely by his grace through the redemption that is in Christ Jesus: whom God hath set forth to be a propitiation through faith in his blood . . . .'

Blood, the blood of the cross. This is the great theme of all these epistles. Read it again in Romans 5. 'For when we were yet without strength, in due time Christ died for the ungodly. For scarcely for a righteous man will one die: yet peradventure for a good man some would even dare to die. But God commendeth his love toward us, in that, while we were yet sinners, Christ died for us. Much more then, being now justified by his blood, we shall be saved from wrath through him.' And on and on I could go, quoting scriptures to you. The Apostle tells the Corinthians in the very first chapter of his first epistle to them: 'For the Jews require a sign, and the Greeks seek after wisdom: but we preach Christ crucified, unto the Jews a stumbling block, and unto the Greeks foolishness . . . .' Not only that, he says in the second chapter, 'For I determined not to know anything among you, save Jesus Christ, and him crucified.' This was his constant sermon, his constant preaching. If you are in any doubt about it, let him summarize it himself at the beginning of 1 Corinthians 15, 'Moreover, brethren, I declare unto you the gospel which I preached unto you, which also ye have received, and wherein ye stand; by which also are ye saved, if ye keep in memory what I preached unto you, unless ye have believed in vain. For I delivered unto you first of all that which I also received ...' What was it? '... how that Christ died for our sins according to the scriptures; and that he was buried, and that he rose again the third day according to the scriptures: ...' but you notice that is the thing he preached most of all, first in importance as well as in time. This was the centre of the message, how that Christ died for our sins.

Paul preached it everywhere; in 2 Corinthians 5, he puts it like this: 'Now then we are ambassadors for Christ ...' I do not speak in my own right, he says. I am not visiting you in my own right or at my own cost. I am a man who is sent. He says this is my whole position: 'Now then we are ambassadors for Christ, as though God did beseech you by us: we pray you in Christ's stead, be ye reconciled to God.' What then is the message? It is that 'God was in Christ, reconciling the world unto himself, not imputing their trespasses unto them; ... he hath made him to be sin for us, who knew no sin; that we might be made the righteousness of God in him.' I must not go on, my friends, though I am tempted to do so. I enjoy reading these glorious scriptures. But what I am trying to establish is that this is the first essential and central message of the preaching of the Christian gospel. Let me, therefore, take you finally to Revelation and the letters to the seven churches which are in Asia: 'Grace be unto you, and peace, from him which is, and which was, and which is to come; and from the seven Spirits which are before his throne; and from Jesus Christ, who is the faithful witness, and the first begotten of the dead, and the prince of the kings of the earth. Unto him that loved us, and washed us from our sins in his own blood.'

There it is then. It is in the whole of the Scriptures. What right have you or anybody else, what right has any ecclesiastic, to get up and pour his scorn upon the blood of Christ, and to say the cross does not matter, that it is the teaching we want, or that it is the imitation of the person that we need? The whole of the New Testament is proclaiming the blood of Christ, the death of Christ upon the cross, on Calvary. It is the heart and centre of the Christian evangel, the good news of salvation.

And finally, if you want further evidence, consider the Communion table, with the plates of broken bread, and the glasses holding wine. Bread and wine, what do they signify? There is only one answer: 'I have received of the Lord,' says Paul, 'that which also I delivered unto you ...' (1 Cor 11:23). It is the command of the Son of God himself. The one who instituted the Last Supper, who had it with his own followers the night before he was crucified. Go on doing this, he said, let my people go on doing it always. Let them come and break bread and drink wine. 'This do in remembrance of me.' And we Christians do this as the Apostle instructs us, that we may declare, proclaim, preach and announce, the Lord's death, till he come. Not his teaching, not his example primarily, but his death. And one of the sacraments has been ordained in order that we might never forget.

Very well, there is our evidence. This is the first and the central thing. That is the Apostle's first reason, therefore, for preaching it. But let me ask a second question. Why does he glory in this? He does so, he tells us, because it is by this cross that we are saved. Paul puts it like this: 'But God forbid that I should glory, save in the cross of our Lord Jesus Christ, by whom the world is crucified unto me, and I unto the world.' *By whom*. Now this is most wonderful. He preached the cross because it is the cross that really does this thing that sets us free, and gives us our salvation. This is absolutely vital. The death of our Lord upon the cross was not an accident, it was not the greatest tragedy of all time, neither was it something that you and I must imitate. These are the things that are preached about it. So often this is what you hear: 'Oh, of course it was an accident. It need not, nor should it, have taken place. Those dull, stupid people, those politically minded Jews, those jealous people, those Pharisees, who could see that he knew more than they did, and could teach better than they did—they were the cause of the trouble. It was all a terrible tragedy. That is why it happened, and it is a great shame that it ever did happen. So let us say as little as we can about it, and praise him and his teaching and his example.'

That is the exact opposite of what the whole of the New Testament says. The cross, the death of our Lord upon the cross, is not something to be regretted. It is not something to be explained away. Nor is it something to be kept out of sight or hidden. 'God forbid that I should glory save in the cross of our Lord Jesus Christ.' Put that in the centre, place it in the front. Proclaim it above everything else, as he has already done in the first verse of the third chapter of this very epistle. He says that he is amazed at the foolish Galatians: 'Who hath bewitched you, that ye should not obey the truth, before whose eyes Jesus Christ hath been evidently set forth'—placarded, enacted in dramatic manner, that is the meaning of 'set forth'. He held it before them that this was the centre and the core of his preaching, because it is by this that we are saved.

So you do not regret the cross, and you do not try to forget it or idealize it, or philosophize about it, and turn it into something beautiful and wonderful. No, what you say is this: I glory in it! Why? Because it is by this that 'the world is crucified unto me, and I unto the world.' It is the means of my salvation. It is the very way in which I am saved. In other words, the Apostle tells us that he preaches this because that which happened there, when our Lord died on that cross, is the very thing that saves us. If he had not died upon the cross, nobody would ever have been saved. There would be no gospel to preach. It is the saving event. It is the act whereby our salvation is accomplished. That is why the Apostle glories in it. That is why Isaac Watts says 'When I survey *the wondrous cross*'. It is the thing which saves us and without which we would not be saved at all.

Again, there is abundant evidence to establish this point. Read at the end of Luke's Gospel what our Lord himself says after his resurrection: 'Then opened he their understanding, that they might understand the scriptures, and said unto them, Thus it is written, and thus it behoved, Christ to suffer, and to rise from the dead the third day: and that repentance and remission of sins should be preached in his name among all nations, beginning at Jerusalem. And ye are witnesses of these things.' And we have seen that Paul, preaching to the people of Antioch, finishes his sermon by saying, 'Be it known unto you, therefore, men and brethren, that through this man is preached unto you the forgiveness of sins: and by him all that believe are justified from all things, from which ye could not be justified by the law of Moses' (Acts 13:38–39). This is the thing whereby we are saved. And the Apostle has already told that to the Galatians at the very beginning of his letter: 'Grace be to you and peace from God the Father, and from our Lord Jesus Christ, who gave himself for our sins, that he might deliver us from this present evil world, according to the will of God and our Father' (1:3–4).

There you have exactly the same thing that he is saying here in the summary at the end. He was always saying it. So the cross is the centre of apostolic preaching because it is the thing that saves us. It does not ask us to save ourselves, it does not tell us to do something that will save us, it says it is done, it has happened, it was happening there. That is the gospel. There is the event which saves us. It is a saving event, that is why he glories in it and that is why he preached it.

That in turn leads me to the next principle which is, 'How does this cross save us?' That is what you want to know, is it not? Any man who is saved, is saved by the cross, and to be saved means that your sins are forgiven, that you are reconciled to God. You become a child of God, and you begin to receive his blessing. You have no fear of death or the grave and the judgement. You know you are going to inherit glory. How then does the cross save us? Here is the question of questions. Let the Apostle answer it in his own words here: 'God forbid that I should glory, save in the cross of our Lord Jesus Christ.'

Look at the cross, my friend. Have you ever really looked at it? Have you ever, with Isaac Watts, surveyed this wondrous cross? I am asking you to do so now. Look at those three crosses on that little hill called Calvary, outside the city of Jerusalem. Look at the middle one and at that person who is dying there. They are amazed that he has died so quickly. Who is he? That is the first question. You will never understand the significance of what happened there until you are clear about who it was that was dying there. Who is this person in the middle nailed to a tree? And the Apostle answers the question: he is our Lord Jesus Christ. Jesus is a man, obviously, you look at him and you can see he is a man like the other two. Ah yes, but *who* is he? He is a carpenter brought up in a place called Nazareth. He worked here until the age of thirty, and then he set out as a preacher. He was an extraordinary prophet, and people said that he had worked miracles. Ah, he is a remarkable man, he is an outstanding religious genius, perhaps a political agitator to boot? Who is this? That is the question.

And the answer is that he is the Lord, which means that he is the Son of God. You remember what he said to Peter at

Caesarea Philippi Peter said, 'Thou art the Christ, the Son of the living God.' You are right, Jesus said, 'Blessed art thou, Simon Bar-jona: for flesh and blood hath not revealed it unto thee, but my Father which is in heaven.' If you were only looking with eyes of flesh you would see nothing in me but a man, but you see more, and you know that I am the Christ of God. It is my Father who has revealed it; that is the truth. Jesus is the Lord of Glory. He is the eternal Son of God. He is the second person in the blessed Holy Trinity. He is God the Son.

But you say, now you land me with another problem. If he is the Son of God what is he doing there on the cross? If you say that this is the eternal Son of God who has come out of eternity into time, and has taken unto him human nature and a human body, why has he died? Why does God die? What is he, of everybody, doing there? How did he come to that? I do not want to waste your time with foolish modern suggestions and ancient suggestions that have been put forward. That is not the death of a pacifist. That is not the death of a good man who was misunderstood or the death of someone who was too weak to assert himself. My dear friend, you are doing violence to him, you are insulting him, it is a libel upon him. What is he doing there? He tells us himself, I have already quoted it to you. 'The Son of Man,' he says, 'came not to be ministered unto, but to minister, and to give his life a ransom for many' (Mt 20:28). He taught them that he had come in order to die. I reminded you of the phrase 'He stedfastly set his face to go to Jerusalem'. His disciples did not understand all this, and they did their utmost to keep him from Jerusalem. We are given the actual record of this very thing. 'The same day there came certain of the Pharisees, saying unto him, Get thee out, and depart hence: for Herod will kill thee. And he said unto them, Go ye, and tell that fox, Behold, I cast out devils, and I do cures today and tomorrow, and the third day I shall be perfected. Nevertheless I must walk to day, and to morrow, and the day following: for it cannot be that a prophet perish out of Jerusalem' (Lk 13:32–33). He knew exactly where he was going, and why he had come into this world.

And there at the very end when he is surrounded by his enemies, and they have confined him to the Garden of Gethsemane, his own disciples become concerned for him and they say, Shall we go out and buy swords? We must defend you at all costs. And one of them drew out his sword and cut off the ear of the high priest's servant, you remember.

Put the swords back, he says. 'Thinkest thou that I cannot now pray to my Father, and he shall presently give me, more than twelve legions of Angels?' He says what do you think I am, and what do you think I am doing? Do you not know that if I wanted to get out of this world without the death of the cross, I have simply to ask my Father and immediately he would give me twelve legions of angels and I would be wafted by angels back into the glory out of which I have come? But, he says, if I do that, how can I fulfil righteousness? How can I do the work that my Father has sent me to do? No, he says that he has come deliberately to die.

Now there is a wonderful statement of all this in Hebrews 2:9, 'We see Jesus, who was made a little lower than the angels'—what for?—'for the suffering of death ...' We see him now, '... crowned with glory and honour; that he by the grace of God should taste death for every man.' My friends, the Son of God is there dying on that cross because he came from heaven into this world in order to die. That is why he came. He was made a little lower than the angels for the suffering of death. He took on human nature in order that he might die. It is not an accident. It is not something to be explained away. It is essential. He came to give his life a ransom for many.

But why did he do this? The answer is here in the whole of the Bible, from beginning to end. It is here in this one verse. He came because you and I and all mankind are guilty and under the condemnation of a Holy God. He came to deliver us from this world which is doomed to disaster and final destruction, 'by whom the world is crucified unto me, and I unto the world.' We all belong to the world. We are men of the world, we are born in the world, and we will bear the world's fate, unless he can deliver us. That is why he did it. Paul, as we have seen, says in Romans 3: 'For all have sinned.' There is no difference, Jew or Gentile, 'For all have sinned, and come short of the glory of God.' All this nonsense about the good men and the bad men, moral and immoral men. It means nothing in the sight of God. I agree it is important from the point of view of the state, but in the sight of God the most respectable non-Christian is as damned and as hopeless as the vilest reprobate and sinner. There is no difference. Respectability does not count with God. Morality is nothing in the sight of God. It is filthy rags, it is nothing. 'All have sinned, and come short of the glory of God.' That is one reason why he came.

Yes, but then you say, Why can God not forgive this, why does the love of God not forgive a man who says he is sorry and who repents? That question, also, is answered in the Bible, and this is why the Son of God died. God, unlike us, is light, and in him is no darkness at all. God is just, God is holy. God is righteous. Of course, that means nothing to us. How can we think of holiness? We, ugly, foul, vile, sinful creatures. No, we do not understand the righteousness of God. That is why modern man does not believe in the blood of the cross. He does not know what righteousness is. He does not know what justice is or what law is. He does not believe in disci- pline, and his world is becoming a hell for that reason. But God is righteous, he is the law giver, he is holy, he is of so

32

pure a countenance that he cannot even look upon sin; and God cannot pretend that he has not seen it. God sees sin. He sees everything. He must punish sin. His own holy nature insists upon it and he has told us abundantly that he is going to do so. So here is the problem. Man is a guilty sinner, God is a holy God. How can the two be brought together? The answer is the cross of Christ.

How is it the answer, says somebody? Let me tell you. I am putting this as plainly, as simply and as briefly as I can. The answer is like this. The wages of sin is death. That is God's own pronouncement. Without shedding of blood there is no remission of sins. If you go back to the Old Testament, what do you find there? Well, you find a great deal about sacrifices for sin. The people take a bullock to the High Priest and he puts his hands upon its head. They then kill the bullock, take its blood and present it before God in the holy place. What are they doing? Well it is God who has told them to do it. But why did he tell them to do it? The answer is that the wages of sin is death and that without the shedding of blood there is no remission of sins. What they were doing, in a picture, was this. By putting their hands on the head of the bullock they were, as it were, transferring their sins to the bullock. The sins were on the bullock. They then killed the bullock and presented his blood as an offering. God taught them to do that. They transferred their guilt to the animal and then the animal was killed and his blood was offered. They did that every day in the Temple. They took a lamb, a pure unblemished lamb, they killed it and took the blood. You remember what happened when the children of Israel were taken out of Egypt—the tremendous night when death came and killed all the first born of the Egyptians, but not the first born of the Israelites. Why? Because they had painted the posts and lintels of their doors with blood. They had taken a lamb and they had slain it and then painted the door posts and the lintels with the blood of the lamb. And they were passed by, their sins were not punished and their lives were saved.

Jesus Christ, the Son of God, comes. Why has he come? John the Baptist who went round before him, he gave the answer. John the Baptist had only got one sermon and he kept on repeating it, and this was it. Behold, he says, I am not he. I am unworthy to undo the laces of his shoes. Behold, behold, behold 'the lamb of God, which taketh away the sin of the world.' All the others were but types and shadows, indications and adumbrations. The Lamb of God has come. God has provided his own sacrifice. It is his own Son. The Lamb of God. This is what happened on Calvary's tree. God took your sins and mine and he put them on the head of his own Son, and then he smote him, he punished him, he struck him, he killed him. The wages of sin is death.

So what was happening on the cross was that God himself was laying your sins and mine upon his own dearly beloved Son, and he paid the penalty of our guilt and our transgressions. 'For he hath made him to be sin for us, who knew no sin; that we might be made the righteousness of God in him' (2 Cor 5:21). 'The Lord hath laid on him the iniquity of us all' (Is 53:6). That is what the Father did. What did the son do? He was passive as a lamb, he did not grumble, he did not complain. He took it all upon him. He allowed it to happen. He surrendered himself deliberately and freely.

Again I remind you how the Apostle puts it. 'Who gave himself for [on behalf of] our sins, that he might deliver us from this present evil world, according to the will of God and our Father' (Gal 1:4). But still more wonderfully, at the end of Galatians 2: 'I through the law, am dead to the law, that I might live unto God. I am crucified with Christ: nevertheless I live; yet not I, but Christ liveth in me: and the life which I now live in the flesh I live by the faith of the Son of

God, who loved me, and gave himself for me.'

That is the gospel. 'For God so loved the world, that he gave—to that death—his only begotten Son, that whosoever believeth in him should not perish, but have everlasting life' (Jn 3:16); 'Who his own self bare our sins in his own body on the tree, that we, being dead to sins, should live unto righteousness: by whose stripes ye were healed' (1 Pet 2:24). That is why it happened, that is the meaning. That is why the Apostle gloried in it. It is the cross of Christ that saves us. He saves us by bearing our punishment and by taking our guilt upon him. God smites him, and the law of God is satisfied. I am dead to the law through the law. The law has been carried out. Carried out upon him, so I am free. 'There is therefore now no condemnation to them which are in Christ Jesus . . . .'

'For God so loved the world, that he gave . . .'; '. . . the Son of God, who loved me, and gave himself for me.' This is the preaching of the cross. It is the cross that saves me. What am I to do? You and I have only one thing to do. I have nothing to do but to believe this message. Nothing else. Do not tell me you are going to live a better life. You have not seen the truth if you say that. Do not tell me you are going to be a better man, or a better woman. Do not tell me that you are going to stop this or that. You have not seen it. You have only one thing to do. 'Be it known unto you therefore, men and brethren, that through this man is preached unto you the forgiveness of sins: and by him all that believe are justified from all things, from which ye could not be justified by the law of Moses' (Acts 13:38–39).

> Only believe [nothing else] and thou shalt see
> That Christ is all in all to thee.

It does not matter what you have been, men and brethren, let me address you as the Apostle addressed these people at

Antioch in Pisidia. I do not know you, my friends, not individually, most of you, but this is the wonderful thing about
the work of a preacher, he does not need to know his congregation. Do you know why? Because I know the most
important thing about every single one of you, and that is
that each of you is a vile sinner. I do not care who you are,
because all have sinned and come short of the glory of God.
I do not care what particular form your sin takes. There is a
great deal of attention paid to that today. The preacher is
not interested in that. I do not want a catalogue of your sins.
I do not care what your sins are. They can be very respectable or they can be heinous, vile, foul, filthy. It does not
matter, thank God. But what I have authority to tell you is
this. Though you may be the vilest man or woman ever
known, and though you may until this moment have lived
your life in the gutters and the brothels of sin in every shape
and form, I say this to you: be it known unto you that
through this man, this Lord Jesus Christ, is preached unto
you the forgiveness of sin. And by him all who believe, you
included, are at this very moment justified entirely and
completely from everything you have ever done—if you
believe that this is the Lord Jesus Christ, the Son of God, and
that he died there on the cross, for your sins and to bear
your punishment. If you believe that, and thank him for it,
and rely utterly only upon him and what he has done, I tell
you, in the name of God, all your sins are blotted out completely, as if you had never sinned in your life, and his
righteousness is put on you and God sees you perfect in his
Son. That is the message of the cross, that is Christian
preaching, that it is our Lord who saves us, by dying on the
cross, and that nothing else can save us, but that that can
save whosoever believeth in him. You remember the Philip-
pian jailer? That violent fellow was about to commit suicide,
and was stopped by Paul. Then he came to the Apostle and

to Silas and said, 'Sirs, what must I do to be saved?' The answer was simply this. 'Believe on the Lord Jesus Christ, and thou shalt be saved, and thy house,' and he believed and he was saved, and he began to rejoice from that very moment (Acts 16:30–31).

My friends, that is why the Apostle glories in the cross of the Lord Jesus Christ. He had a message that he could take throughout the world, to the blackest and the vilest and the most hopeless of men and, equally to the respectable and all the good and the nice and the kind. He could take it to all men. And he had the same message for them all, that they were all lost and dead, but that whosoever believed in this message was immediately justified. Very well, I put it before you exactly as the Apostle did in Antioch of Pisidia. I want to ask you a question and this is it. When the Jews were gone out of the synagogue, the Gentiles besought that these words might be preached to them on the next Sabbath. They wanted to hear more about it. Do you? Do you want to hear more about it? I am going on with this great theme, and I am going to test you. If you have had even a glimmer of an inkling into this truth you will want to hear more about it. But if you do not want to hear more about it, let me warn you in the words of the Apostle. 'Beware, therefore, lest that come upon you, which is spoken of in the prophets; behold, ye despisers, and wonder, and perish: for I work a work in your days, a work which ye shall in no wise believe, though a man declare it unto you' (Acts 13:41). Tell me, do you glory in the cross of our Lord Jesus Christ? Would you willingly and gladly spend all your days in singing the praise of this Son of God who loved you and gave himself for you? Let us examine ourselves. Let every man and woman answer for himself and for herself.

Let us, then, finish with the answer which Charles Wesley gave two hundred years ago:

THE CROSS

And can it be that I should gain
An interest in the Saviour's blood!
Died He for me who caused His pain?
For me, who Him to death pursued?
Amazing love! how can it be
That Thou, my God, shouldst die for me!

Chapter 2

The Acid Test

'But God forbid that I should glory, save in the cross of our Lord Jesus Christ, by whom the world is crucified unto me and I unto the world.'

As we come back to this great theme, it is important that we should bear in mind the context, the way in which the apostle Paul intends to make the statement. In reading the text, we must put an emphasis upon the word 'I'. 'But God forbid that *I* should glory, save in the cross of our Lord Jesus Christ.' The Apostle is contrasting himself with certain other people—with the false Judaizing teachers who had been speaking and preaching to the churches in Galatia after Paul's departure, and who had been causing such confusion in the minds of those simple people with respect to the way of salvation.

The Apostle says about them 'For neither they themselves who are circumcised keep the law; but desire to have you circumcised, that they may glory in your flesh' (v.13). That is what they glory in. But as for me, says the Apostle, out upon the suggestion that I should glory in anything, save in the cross of our Lord Jesus Christ. This is the one thing and the only thing in which I glory. That is a tremendous statement, of course. And we realize that if we are to be able to say the same, we must know something about the things which he tells us. Our desire to know more shows the sincerity of our concern. As he ends his letter, he gives them a solemn warning to be very careful. He says, 'For he that soweth to the flesh shall of the flesh reap corruption; but he that soweth to the Spirit shall of the Spirit reap life everlasting' (6:8).

So the great question for us is, how does one sow to the Spirit? And it is just here that these false teachers were creating such trouble, and are still causing trouble in the same way to many people in the modern world. That is precisely why I am calling attention to this whole subject. People are asking, 'What are we to believe? What is this Christian faith? We are hearing contradictory statements,' they say. That is what they were saying in Galatia. The Apostle Paul had said one thing; these teachers were saying something different. Paul said you must believe in Jesus Christ and him crucified *only*, you are justified by faith *only*. No, said the others, it is by circumcision. You must go back to the law. So here were people in confusion, and they are, as I pointed out, in confusion today. Nothing is more necessary than that we should be perfectly clear about our authority, and there are only two ultimate authorities: the Bible, or anything else you like. There is no other choice. Everybody bases his opinion either upon this book or else not upon it. I do not care what it is if it is not on this. There are many possibilities apart from this, it does not matter, because they are all the same in that they are not the Bible.

Well now then, says Paul, what is the truth? What is the real message? It is the cross of our Lord Jesus Christ: 'Jesus Christ and him crucified'. The preaching of the cross, as we have seen, is the heart and centre of the whole Christian position; not our Lord's teaching but the cross—his death. Why? Because it is by this that we are saved.

Now there is the matter in general, but as it is such a tremendous statement, we cannot leave it at that. The Apostle does not merely say that he preaches the cross and that he believes in it. He says, 'God forbid that I should *glory*, save in the cross of our Lord Jesus Christ.' So there is more here, and it is to something of this 'more' that I want to draw your attention now.

This word 'glory' tells us at once that the cross of our Lord Jesus Christ is the test of every one of us. It is the test of our profession of Christianity. It is the test of our church membership, indeed, of our whole position and profession. There is no more subtle test of our understanding than our attitude to the cross of our Lord Jesus Christ. In other words, the cross passes judgement upon us all, immediately and of necessity. You cannot remain neutral in the presence of the cross. It has always divided mankind and it still does. And what the Apostle says is that there are ultimately only two positions with respect to it. The cross of our Lord Jesus Christ is either an offence to us or else it is the thing above everything else in which we glory.

My dear friends, there never can be a more important question than this: what does this cross do to you? Where do you find yourself as you think of it and face it? It is one of these two, it is either an offence or else you glory in it. Are we all clear about our position? Do we know exactly where we stand? There are some perhaps saying, 'Well quite certainly it is not an offence to me, but I am afraid I cannot say I glory in it.' Well, my friend, you are in an impossible position. These are the only two positions—offence, or glory. As we value our immortal souls, let us examine this matter, let us look into it, let us see what the Apostle has got to tell us here, and elsewhere in his writings, about these two positions, in order that we may know for sure.

Now this is important for this reason. Paul's preaching, as

we have seen, is this: It is the cross that saves me, by whom or by which the world is crucified unto me and I unto the world. He says to the Corinthians, 'I determined not to know anything among you, save Jesus Christ, and him crucified' (1 Cor 2:2). The Apostle Paul never delivered a lecture. He always preached. And the business of the Christian church is to preach, not to lecture. It is not to deal with politics, nor with social conditions but to preach. 'I determined not to know anything among you ...'—and what a vast knowledge he possessed! All the erudition of this mighty man of God, all his profound understanding, all his knowledge of philosophy and of Greek poetry and a thousand and one other things—and he determined to become a fool for Christ's sake.

It was even brought as a charge against him. That man Paul, they said, was always speaking about this cross, always about the blood of Christ. It was so simple, it was even childish. He did not take his hearers, they said, into the heights of philosophic understanding.

The Apostle answers and says that that was all deliberate: 'I *determined* not to know anything among you, save ....' I know of a wisdom, he says to the Corinthians, 'Howbeit we speak wisdom among them that are perfect: yet not the wisdom of this world, nor of the princes of this world, that come to nought' (1 Cor 2:6). It is a hidden wisdom. It is a mystery. It is the wisdom of God.

Now the Apostle came to that position for this one big reason. Here is the thing that determines not only the kind of life we live in this world, but that determines our eternal destiny. 'He that soweth to the Spirit shall of the Spirit reap life everlasting.' The thing is terribly urgent, more than ever in this so called atomic age world, which may come to an end at any moment. And there before us is eternity. Where are you going to spend it, as the old preachers used to put it?

42

Do you know what determines that? Your reaction to the cross. This is the acid test. This is the thing that searches us out of all our hiding and lurking places. This demands a decision urgently, because we are in either one or other of the two positions. Which is it?

Now let us follow the Apostle as he puts this thing before us. Let me put it to you in the form of some principles. Here is the first. To the non-Christian, the cross is an offence. Now I take that word from Galatians 5:11 where the Apostle says, 'And I, brethren, if I yet preach circumcision, why do I yet suffer persecution? then is the offence of the cross ceased.' In other words, he is saying that the preaching of the cross is an offence to the natural man, to the man who is not a Christian. There is no doubt at all that that was the position in the early days. We have abundant evidence with respect to it. He says it here, and in 1 Corinthians 1:23 he says I know perfectly well that preaching Christ crucified is 'unto the Jews a stumblingblock, and unto the Greeks foolishness.' They do not like it, they do not want it, it is an offence to them. And he was persecuted by his own countrymen and laughed at and dismissed by the learned Greeks, because he persisted in preaching this message of the cross.

It was, then, clearly and patently an offence in the early days of the Christian church, and so it has continued to be throughout the running centuries. There has been great argument and disputation about the cross. There has always been trouble about it. This has been the dividing point so constantly through the ages. And it is still the same tonight. The fact that the cross is an offence to large numbers at the present time is only too obvious and too patent. There is scorn being poured upon it, even in the Christian church. This theology of blood, they say. How they hate any mention of the *blood*.

I remember once listening to some men in discussion. A

Christian and a non-Christian were talking together about these matters, and I was sitting in an adjoining room reading, when suddenly the Christian came to me and said, 'Come, I think you can help us with this discussion.'

So I went along with him and asked what the problem was.

The other man, the non-Christian, who was a very able professional man, said, 'You know, there is a dispute here, but there shouldn't be.'

'What do you mean?' I asked.

'Well,' he said, 'it is my good friend here. Of course I believe in morals as he does. I believe in ethics. I believe in living a good life. I believe in improving this world, but,' he continued, 'he will bring in this blood and thunder element.'

That was the cause of the trouble, what he called 'blood and thunder'. What men call 'this theology of blood'. They pour their scorn and their ridicule upon it. They hate the Old Testament, they hate what they call the God sitting on Mount Sinai, they hate all this offering of burnt offerings and sacrifices. They say that is primitive religion, and you should not introduce it into the discussion, you should not talk about such things. They hate the cross, it is an offence still, to the polite, the sophisticated, the dilettante, the modern man.

But perhaps the people who find the cross most offensive of all are those who on the surface seem to praise it most of all. I am thinking of the people who tell us that the cross is a very beautiful thing. They preach a lot about the cross, yes, but they preach it as something that is beautiful—so touching, so affecting, so moving. And yet I would say that they, of all people, are the ones who feel the offence of the cross most of all. In fact, they feel it so much that they have got to turn it into something that it was never meant to be. They find it so offensive in its stark reality, that they philosophize

it into the most beautiful thing, a kind of aesthetic enact-
ment, and so they sentimentalize the cross and talk about it
with great pathos. These, of all people, are the ones who feel
the offence of the cross.

The truth is that we are face to face with the very position
that has persisted throughout the centuries. We must examine the reasons for this, but before we do so, let me say
this. The test of whether someone is teaching the cross
rightly or wrongly is whether it is an offence to the natural
man or not. If my preaching of this cross is not an offence to
the natural man, I am misrepresenting it. If it is something
that makes him say how beautiful, how wonderful, what a
tragedy, what a shame, I have not been preaching the cross
truly. The preaching of the cross is an offence to the natural
man. So it becomes the test of any man's preaching.

Or let me put it in terms of the congregation. If this element of offence in the cross has never appeared to you, or if
you have never felt it, well then I say that you likewise have
never known the truth about the cross of Christ. If you have
never reacted against it, and felt that it is an offence for you,
I say you have never known it. It is *always* an offence to the
natural man. Invariably, there is no exception. So if you have
never felt it, you have never seen it, because you were once
a natural man. There is nobody born a Christian into this
world. We have to be born again to become Christians, and
while we are natural men and women, the cross is an
offence.

So, if we have never known this element of offence, either
we have not seen it, or we have had some misrepresentation
of it, and that brings me to the next question. Why, then, is it
an offence to the natural man? In what respects is it an
offence to him? The answer is, that the reasons are precisely
those that used to make it an offence to men and women in
the first century. I am sorry, but I have to repeat that there is

45

no difference at all in these matters between the first century man and the twentieth century man. Is that in itself an offence to you? It is a part of the preaching of the cross to say that man in every century is identical with man in every other century. That is a most offensive thing to twentieth century man. Let me show you why.

First and foremost it is an offence to his mind. I have to put this first, because man's ultimate sin is intellectual pride. And this preaching of the cross is an offence to man's mind, because it cuts across all his preconceived notions and ideas and prejudices. It was a stumbling block to the Jews for this reason. They would tell you, We are expecting the Messiah, and, as Jews, our idea of the Messiah is that when he comes he will be a great military personage. He will collect a great army, which he will head, and, he will destroy the Roman conquerors. He will set up Jerusalem as the greatest city in the world and we the Jews will be the greatest people. We shall conquer the whole world, and we shall be there reigning over all. That is what they expected. At first, when he came and they listened to him, they were rather attracted to him. He seemed to have understanding, and power, and they crowded after him. But they soon lost patience with him. He would not go up to Jerusalem and become a king. On one occasion his own followers tried to take him by force to make him a king, and he had to escape to a mountain himself alone. They all thought of him in these military terms.

So when they found the one who claimed to be the Messiah dying in apparent weakness and helplessness upon the cross, they were deeply wounded and offended. They felt that this was nonsense, ridiculous. A Saviour, a deliverer, dying? He ought to be killing everybody else. He ought to be powerful and mighty, a great king and conqueror. He was an offence to them. He had demolished their preconceived notions and ideas. And it was exactly the same with the

Greeks, these men who trusted to their own ability and were so proud of it. This cross cuts across it, does not make any use of it, indeed, as I am going to show you, it does the exact opposite.

So immediately, the cross is an offence, because it cuts across all our ideas. We all have ideas about everything, including religion. We think we know what makes a man a Christian. We think we know what God expects, and we are quite confident that we can do it, that we have it in us. If we only put our backs and our wills into it, we can do it. Is that not it? The cross cuts right across it.

Let me show you how. The second respect in which it is an offence to the mind of the natural man is tremendously important at the present time, even as it was with the Greeks of old. The cross proclaims at once that we are not saved by ideas. We are not saved by thought, or by understanding. We are not saved, if you like, by philosophy. But that is the one thing that the natural man believes—that we are saved in this manner. Who is going to save us? Well, the wise men. And who are they? The wise men are the great thinkers. The country is in trouble, in an awful mess. What can be done? Well, we want the best men, the best thinkers in every realm—political, philosophical, social and in every other respect. The best men, the greatest thinkers, are going to be our salvation. That is how man thinks instinctively. But here is something that tells us that we are not saved by thinking. We are not saved by good ideas. We are not saved by idealism. The most bitter opponents of the cross of Christ in this country today are the idealists who are not Christians. You see, they have their noble ideas, their thoughts about uplift, and what needs to be done, and so do the great profound philosophers. These are the important people, the world says, and they hate the cross, because it cuts right across what they believe.

47

And then another way in which the cross offends the natural man's mind is this: people say, and they say it quite freely, that this whole notion of the cross is immoral. To them, the idea that one man should be punished for other people's sin is immoral. The whole notion is quite unthinkable. A man bears his own punishment. This idea that somebody else comes along who is absolutely innocent, and that you put your guilt on him and that he then bears the punishment—the thing is quite immoral. They say they cannot believe in a God who does a thing like that, a God who can punish his own Son, cause his death, in order to forgive others. It is not justice. They say that it violates their sense of justice and of morality. Have you not heard that? Perhaps you have thought it? If you have, the cross is an offence, because the essence of this doctrine is substitution. It teaches that Christ is the Lamb of God 'that taketh away the sins of the world'; that our sins are transferred to him, are imputed to him, are put upon him; and that it is 'by his stripes we are healed'. It teaches that God has smitten him. God has 'laid on him the iniquity of us all' (Is 53:6). And to the modern man, the natural human thinker, this is an offence, immoral, unjust, and unrighteous. So he hates it and he rejects it.

Perhaps we need to sum up the whole position with regard to the way in which the cross is an offence to the mind of the natural man. What he cannot really endure is that he cannot understand the cross, and that is its essential offence to him. The natural man believes he can understand everything, and he wants to do so. I am sure that you recognize his favourite position, which goes something like this: I am not going to believe a thing which I cannot understand. I am not going to commit myself to anything unless I understand it. Man believes that he has the capacity in himself to comprehend all truth. He can understand everything. He does not believe in God because, he says, he does not understand such a being, and he does not understand the cross either. And of course the cross cannot be understood. As Charles Wesley puts it in a great hymn, 'Tis mystery all, the immortal dies'. The cross is a mystery, the mystery of substitution, of the immortal dying. It is the mystery of God, as the Bible itself says, but the modern man says he cannot submit to a mystery. He must understand. But here is something that tells him you cannot understand. It is impossible. It is beyond us. It is divine. It is miraculous, it is supernatural and we cannot understand it. And man hates it for that reason. He cannot leave it alone because it is there, and because he has a feeling within him somewhere that he will have to deal with it sometime, and yet because he cannot understand it he hates it; it is an offence to him.

And if it is an offence to the natural man's mind, it is still more an offence to his heart. The truth is that there is only one ultimate trouble with respect to the cross, and that is our pride. All man's troubles emanate from his pride. Why did man ever fall? The answer is pride. The devil came to Eve and said, Has God said that you must not eat of that? Of course he has said that, because he knows that the moment you eat of it you will become like God. And the woman liked the suggestion. Pride rose and the man listened. He agreed. They wanted to be as God. What was the cause of the fall of the one who tempted them, the devil? Paul tells us in his first epistle to Timothy that it was exactly the same thing. He lifted himself up in pride, and fell. Pride is the cause of all our troubles and that is what the world does not understand. It is not surprising. Everything is telling us to believe in ourselves, pandering to our pride, building us up and inflating us. Man, modern man! Here comes something that smashes the idol. Pride is ever the cause of the trouble and there is nothing that so hurts the natural man's pride as the cross of Christ.

How does the cross do that? What has happened that there should ever have been a cross? It is because we are failures, because we are sinners, because we are lost. You know, the astounding thing that we are told in the four Gospels is that the Son of God, when he came into this world, was hated, and not only that, but that he was crucified on a cross. Have you ever thought of that? The Son of God came into the world as he said himself, not to condemn it, but that the world through him might be saved. What harm did he do? He spent his time in teaching, instructing the common people and others who were ready to listen. He spent his time in healing sickness and diseases, relieving suffering and pain and sorrow. He spent his time, as Peter puts it to Cornelius, in doing good. And yet they hated him, and they crucified him. And the mob cried out saying, 'Away with him, crucify him!' Why were they upset by him? What had he done to them?

You know the cause of the trouble? He said one thing that to the natural man is the greatest insult conceivable, the most offensive remark that can ever be made, and it was this. 'The Son of man is come to seek and to save that which was lost' (Lk 19:10). But surely, you may think, they did not hate that. Yet they did. That is the very thing they hated him for. They did not object to the saving part, but to the suggestion that they were lost, and that they were lost in the sense that they needed to be saved. You see, the very presence of the Son of God in this world is an utter, absolute condemnation of us, every one of us. It is because all have sinned and come short of the glory of God, that he ever came, and especially why he had to go to the cross. And this is a source of offence. He tells us that we are failures, that we are sinners.

But then he says more. This is another aggravation of the offence. He says that we are all failures. He says that we are all *equally* failures. Now that is utterly impossible to us, is it not? What do we say? Well, what we say in our better moments is, 'I don't claim that I am a hundred per cent saved, you know, but I am not like that hopeless drunkard, I am not like that fallen woman. There are good and bad in this world. There are religious and non-religious people, and there is a very important distinction here. You must not say,' we argue, 'that all people are in the same position. You must not say that it makes no difference whether a man is good or bad or whether a man is moral or immoral, whether a man has an ethical code or whether he has not. You must not say that.' We go on 'You are violating every moral principle. You are asking for licence, for abandon. The thing is a lie, it is not true. You tell us that the man who has striven to live a good life and has tried to be religious and to say his prayers, you say that he is in the same position as a man who has never prayed, has never been near a place of worship, and has lived only for sin and evil, and vice and lust, you say they are in the same lost condition?'

That is precisely what the cross of Christ says.

The cross of Christ says there is no difference. This was the thing, of course, that infuriated the Jews. But this is how the Apostle puts it in Romans 3, in writing on this very matter. 'But now,' he says, 'the righteousness of God without the law is manifested, being witnessed by the law and the prophets; even the righteousness of God which is by faith of Jesus Christ unto all and upon all them that believe: for there is *no difference*. For *all* have sinned, and come short of the glory of God' (3:21–23, italics added). This was the thing that made them mad. They were mad with our Lord, they were mad with the apostles, who preached that there was really no difference between the Jew and the Greek in this matter of salvation; that the fact that you are a Jew does not save you, nor the fact that you have been circumcised, nor that you have got possession of the law. There is no difference between the Jew and the Gentile, the outsider, none at all. All have sinned, there is no difference.

And this is the thing that hurts the pride of modern man in our own day. The world is full of do-gooders. These people are anxious to put things right. They set up an organization, they form a society and other people join it and they write protests and they are going to put the world right. And there is one thing they hate. It is this cross, which tells them that you can never deal with the problem like that, and that all are in the same position. There is no difference, there is none righteous, no, not one. It is a terrible thing to be told that all your effort comes to nothing. Let me put that in this form. The cross is an offence to the pride of the natural man, because it says that not only are we all sinners, not only are we all equally sinners, but it tells us that we are all equally helpless. We can do nothing at all. It tells us that all our righteousness is but as filthy rags. All we regard as best is dung and refuse, and absolutely useless. And it tells us, who believe in ourselves and in our capacity, that we can do nothing. That we are utterly and completely helpless and entirely hopeless. And here it offends us and it hurts us, it damns all our efforts, it is an offence to the mind and to the heart. And it is equally an offence to the will of man. It tells him: I do not care what your will is, I do not care how powerful your will. I do not care what your resolutions are. Do all you will, you will never save yourself.

> Not the labours of my hands
> Can fulfil thy law's demands;
> Could my zeal no respite know,
> Could my tears forever flow,
> All for sin could not atone,
> Thou must save, and thou alone.
>
> *A. M. Toplady*

It crushes us to the ground. It demolishes everything that we have ever believed in. It leaves us helpless and hopeless, lost, damned, hell-deserving sinners, and that is what it says about every one of us.

And, I say, that *that* is the offence of the cross to the natural man. Have you ever felt it, my friend? Have you resented being told that your condition is such that nothing that you can do can ever put it right? Have you ever been told, or been offended by being told, that you are lying there helpless on the ground in dust and ashes and the final hope-lessness, and that although you get up and try to shake your-self and to reform yourself, you will be down again, and in the end you will be down and hopeless and outcast? Have you been able to hear that without feeling the offence, and a hatred towards it? If you have, I would say that you have never heard it properly. There is something wrong with you. The modern man, the natural man, hates this. It is the opposite of his cult of self-expression and belief in himself, of working himself up psychologically, of trusting himself, and of trusting his own innate powers. Modern man con-siders himself come of age, able to stand on his own feet, with all his tremendous knowledge. But here is something that demolishes it all. The cross says that it is useless and of no value at all. That is the offence of the cross to the natural man.

But now, turn to the other side. The Christian, by contrast, is, as we saw earlier, one who glories in the cross. 'God forbid that I should glory, save in the cross of our Lord Jesus Christ.' Let us look at this. This is the important thing for us. You notice what he says. He does not merely say that he admires it, that the cross is simply beautiful and marvellous. No, he does not stand there just admiring it, or merely prais-ing it. I want to go further, he does not just believe it. He does not merely accept its message intellectually. I am going to test you, my friends. The Christian is a man who does not only believe in the cross, he glories in it!

What do you mean by that, says someone? Well, I mean the same as the writer of the hymn when he says:

> In the Cross of Christ I glory,
>   Towering o'er the wrecks of time;
> All the light of sacred story
>   Gathers round its head sublime.
>
> *J. Bowring*

He rejoices in it. The word that the Apostle actually uses here, is a very strong one. He says 'God forbid that I should *boast*'. It is a matter of boasting. He makes his boast of it. He says these Jews are the people who want to have you circumcised, in order that they may boast about their converts. They want to boast in your flesh. They are out for their own success and their own name. They boast in that and they boast about what they have done. Oh, says the Apostle, I boast in nothing, and God forbid that I should, save in the cross of Christ. What he means by that is that he not only admires it, he not only believes in it, he is moved by it. He is captivated by it. He says here, 'God forbid that I should glory, *save* . . .'

In other words, the Christian not only glories in the cross, he glories in the cross *alone*. He glories in nothing else. Hear Isaac Watts putting it:

> Forbid it, Lord, that I should boast
> Save in the death of Christ my God.

There is an exclusiveness about it, which means that to the Christian this is the chiefest thing in history, the most important event that has ever taken place. It means that to him there is nothing which comes anywhere near it in significance. It means that he rests everything upon this, that this means all to him, that he is what he is because of this. He glories in it. I want to ask a question to all Christian believers. Are you glorying in the cross? Or are you just saying, Of course, I always believe, I always have believed, I was brought up to. Can you speak like that about the cross? The test of the Christian is that he glories in it, he exults in it, he boasts of it. It is everything to him, without it he has nothing. He owes all to this, this cross is the centre of his universe in every respect. That is what is meant by boasting.

So, then, let me just ask my final question for the moment. Why does the Christian glory in the cross? There are many answers to that question. First of all, he glories in it because of what he sees in it, or, if you prefer it, he glories in it because of what it shows him. Now here, it seems to me, is the key to the whole matter. I must quote Isaac Watts again because I think he makes this clear. He says, 'When I *survey* the wondrous Cross', and I do not think any man glories in it until he has surveyed it. If you take a casual glance at it, you say, 'Yes I believe in it', but my dear friend these men have been moved! Listen to Watts, listen to Charles Wesley, listen to all of them. These men have really seen the meaning of the cross. They cannot contain themselves, they cannot express themselves. Why? The only secret is that they have been surveying it and looking at it, they have been gazing at it. And you see this is a very good test. How much time do you spend in thinking about the cross, in looking at it, in gazing upon it, in surveying it from all its angles?

> When I survey the wondrous Cross,
>   On which the Prince of glory died,
> My richest gain I count but loss,
>   And pour contempt on all my pride.

He looks at it and he keeps on doing so. Ah, it is what he sees that makes him glory in it.

What does he see? What a question. Let me tell you the first part of the answer. The Christian glories in the cross because he sees there the most amazing spectacle that the world has ever seen, or ever can see. We are living in an age that is very fond of spectacles, in the sense of some remarkable happenings and events, some great show. And the Christian glories in the cross as a spectacle, because the more he looks at the cross the more he sees the glory of God being revealed to him. It displays to him the glory of the triune God, God the Father, God the Son, God the Holy Spirit. He sees all that shining down upon him.

What do you mean? asks someone. Well, let us look at it simply like this. He looks at that cross and he sees a man hanging upon it. Who is he? The answer is, as Watts reminds us, the Prince of Glory. 'When I survey the wondrous cross, on which the Prince of Glory died.' And the Christian sees there these extraordinary series of paradoxes, the most amazing paradoxes that the world ever has known or ever can know. It is almost impossible to describe these. I must call upon another poet to help me. Thank God that they have seen it and said it.

Read what Charles Wesley says about it. ''Tis mystery all.' Why? Well, he says, 'the immortal dies.' Now there is a spectacle. The immortal, the one who is life and in whom is life, the everlasting, the eternal, from eternity. 'In the beginning was the Word, and the Word was with God, and the Word was God' (Jn 1:1). He is immortal, he is everlasting. But the immortal dies! Where is a spectacle like that to be found in this whole universe?

Or take it in the way in which the apostle Peter put it to the Jews in the sermon he preached after he and John had healed the impotent man at the Beautiful Gate of the temple. He says, Do you know what you have done? You have killed the Prince of life. You have killed the author of life. You have killed the beginner and controller of life. Now this is what a Christian sees. He can say, I look there at a man, but I know he is not only man, he is God-man, he is God the eternal Son, who has come down on earth to dwell. He is the author of everything, he made everything, and he sustains everything. But I see him dying. What is this? Oh, it is the killing of the Prince of life.

How difficult it is to put this, but you will agree that the modern man gets very moved by spectacles. He gets very moved and very thrilled by acts of self-abasement and humiliation. He looks at his drama on the television, perhaps some great king pretending to be a nobody in order to do good, and he says, how moving, how wonderful, how uplifting. Oh it is thrilling. He glories in it. But look at this—the Prince of life being killed. ''Tis mystery all, the immortal dies.'

But there are other strange things that meet together at this cross.

> See from his head, his hands, his feet
> Sorrow and love flow mingled down.

What a mixture: love and sorrow. Do you see it? 'Did e'er such love and sorrow meet?' Surely that is a challenge, is it not? You who are expert in drama, and in art, and in music that can move people, here is the question that the cross asks you. Did ever such love and sorrow meet together or flow mingling down together? No, it is unique. This is the spectacle of spectacles, the spectacle of the ages. Listen to another:

> Or thorns compose so rich a crown.

You do not associate crowns and thorns, do you? They are opposites, as it were. The glory and the splendour and the sparkle of a crown and a crown of thorns, fit only to be burnt away, cast away out of sight. But here they come together, 'thorns compose so rich a crown'.

Again, what do I see there? I see one who is sinless, who has never sinned, who gives perfect obedience to his Father in all things. He has never done anybody any wrong, he is innocent, pure and clean. He is altogether without sin. But I see the sinless one being punished. I see one who is utterly and entirely innocent dying for those who are evil and vile and unworthy. Dying for sinners, dying for rebels, dying for his own enemies. I see, over and above this, the one who from eternity had looked into the face of his Father. 'In the beginning was the Word, and the Word was with God ...', which means that the Word, the Son, was looking into the face of God eternally, and here on earth he always pleased his Father. He prayed to his Father and looked into his face. I see one who has ever looked into the face of his heavenly Father, his Father, God, in the blessed Holy Trinity. I see that same person crying out in agony, 'My God, my God, why hast thou forsaken me?' That is what I see there at the cross. These endless paradoxes, these things that appear to be utter contradictions, all blending together, becoming one, with a radiance and a glory upon them.

Then I see something else, too. I see the Lord of Glory, the 'Word' by whom all things were made and without whom was nothing made that was made. I see the one who has such power that he can make all things, and indeed, as the author of the epistle to the Hebrews reminds us, the one by whom all things consist and who is 'upholding all things by the word of his power', holding the atoms together, holding the constellations, holding the whole cosmos together, by his power, I see him dying in utter helplessness, in apparent weakness. You remember how it was hurled in his face, 'He saved others; himself he cannot save' (Mt 27:42). You who can heal the sick, and raise the dead, come down. He did not come down. The power and the helplessness are there together and at the same time. I read of the one in whom we are told 'in him was life', dying. That is what I see as I look at the cross. I see one who was 'in the form of God' (Phil 2:6) dying as a weak and helpless man.

I see one whose concern for the glory of his Father was so great that he put aside his own eternal glory in its visible form, and humbled himself, and made himself of no reputation but took upon him the form and the likeness of a man. He indeed took upon him the form and the likeness of a servant, and humbled himself and was obedient, even unto death. That is what I see, his concern for his Father's glory. I see his obedience which was an obedience even unto the death of the cross. 'O my Father,' he said, 'if it be possible, let this cup pass from me: nevertheless not as I will, but as thou wilt.' And he drank it to the very dregs. What was that? Your guilt and mine, your punishment and mine. He took it all upon himself. Why? So that God may be glorified and that God may be just over all. He rendered this perfect obedience that he might honour and glorify his Father.

But looking again at him what I see above everything else is the love that made him do it all. 'Love so amazing, so divine.' What does it mean? Let the Apostle himself answer the question. This is how he puts it. 'For when we were yet without strength, in due time Christ died for the ungodly. For scarcely for a righteous man will one die: yet peradventure for a good man some would even dare to die. But God commendeth his love toward us, in that, while we were yet sinners, Christ died for us. Much more then, being now justified by his blood, we shall be saved from wrath through him. For if, when we were enemies, we were reconciled to God by the death of his Son, much more, being reconciled, we shall be saved by his life' (Rom 5:6–10).

It comes to this, my dear friends, he is dying there because of his love, his love for you, his love for me; his love for those who are sinners, those who are rebels, those who are enemies. He died for people who hated him. As he was dying there, Saul of Tarsus was hating him, but he was dying for Saul of Tarsus. As Paul (to give his subsequent name) puts it later: 'The Son of God, who loved me, and gave himself for me' (Gal 2:20). He did not wait until Paul was converted before he loved him. He loved him as he was, a blasphemer and persecuter and injurious. He loved him even when Saul of Tarsus was there blaspheming his holy name, ridiculing his claim that he was the Son of God, and the Lord of Glory, ridiculing this idea that he is here to teach us and to die for us and to save us, pouring his blasphemous scorn upon him. While Paul was doing that, he was dying for Paul. And he was doing the same for you and for me. You who have reviled him and blasphemed him and hated him and regarded all this preaching of the cross as an offence, he did it for *you*. That is the measure of his love. When I survey the wondrous cross, what do I see? That is what I see. I see a spectacle that the world has never seen before, and will never see again. I see the holy Son of God bearing the punishment of my sins, the author of life dying that I might live, that I might become a son, a child of God, and go on to spend my eternity in the glory everlasting with him.

And this is only the beginning. I say that what we see in the cross is the glory of the Godhead shining down upon us, first in the face of Jesus Christ. Have you seen it? If you have seen even a glimmer of what I have been trying to say, you must glory in it. You do not just believe it, you do not just praise it. You say,

> Love so amazing, so divine,
> Demands my soul, my life, my all.

A total allegiance, a total surrender. I live for him; he died for me. In other words, we put it, as the famous Count

Zinzendorf, the great Moravian leader put it. It was the turning point in his life when he saw that portrait of Christ with its little inscription, 'Christ dying on the cross'. He looked at the picture, he, the wealthy and learned Count, and this is what he read: 'I did this for thee, what wilt thou do for me?' He saw that there was only one response, and for the rest of his life this was his confession: 'I have but one passion, it is he and he alone.'

'God forbid that I should glory, save in the cross of the Lord Jesus Christ . . . .'

Do you really believe that the Son of God came down from heaven and died on that cross for you? Do you really believe it? You cannot truly believe it without glorying in it. If you really believe it and see what it means, well, it is everything to you. It is either everything or else it is nothing. Are you glorying in the cross, my friend? If you are, you can take it from me that you have sown, and are sowing, to the Spirit and that you will reap life everlasting.

Chapter 3

The Wisdom of God

'God forbid that I should glory, save in the cross of our Lord Jesus Christ, by whom the world is crucified unto me, and I unto the world.' We have yet more to say about this great and most wonderful statement. The Apostle here is nailing his colours to the mast, if you like, and making a great declaration of his own personal position. He is contrasting himself with certain false teachers who glory and make their boast in the flesh, interested in themselves and in their own success and the use that they can make of other people. The Apostle says God forbid that he should be interested in, or glory in, anything like that. He glories in nothing, he boasts in nothing, save in the cross of the Lord Jesus Christ.

We have seen that the cross is the very heart and centre of the Christian message, a historical event with which we are confronted, and we have seen, too, that our eternal destiny depends upon the view we take of the death of Jesus of Nazareth upon that cross. So we have been considering why the Christian says that the cross of Christ, the death of this Son of God upon the cross, is to him the most momentous, the most vital of all facts, that there is nothing that compares with it, and that to him it is the most significant thing in the universe.

I put that point deliberately. The Christian is a man who says, I do not care what has happened; I do not care what may happen. I do not care what it is—atomic bombs, or anything you like. For me, nothing can ever approach in significance to the thing that happened there on the cross when Jesus of Nazareth died and was buried in the grave and rose again, and went back to the glory everlasting. Why does the Christian say this? Why does he make his boast in the cross? Why does he glory in it? We have begun to answer that question. We have seen that the cross, with all its mighty paradoxes, is a spectacle which makes anything that you can think of in history, or anything that you can imagine, simply pale into insignificance. But now, we must proceed, because you cannot see a thing like that and leave it there. You must ask a question. Why did he do that? You are quite entitled to ask, for you will say, if that is true, why did it ever happen? And that is a good question. But there is only one way of answering it. Let us look again at the cross. Let us survey it once more. When a man like the apostle Paul glories in the cross you can be quite sure, my friend, that it is the biggest and the deepest and the profoundest thing in the whole universe. A casual glance at the cross is not enough. The saints of the centuries have been surveying it, they have been looking at it, gazing upon it, and meditating upon it. And the more they look at it the more they see in it. The writers of the hymns have done the same thing. The cross of Christ has produced some of the most magnificent poetry in the English language. But the writers have looked at it, they have surveyed it, they have not just said, 'Oh yes, I know Jesus died, he was a pacifist, and he died'—and then gone on indifferently. Neither have they said something like some of us perhaps—Christian people, evangelical people— 'Oh yes, I believe in the cross, I believe Christ died for me', and then thought no more about it. Oh, my dear friend, if that is how if affects you, you have not seen the cross. You must stop and look, survey, put everything else on one side and gaze at it, and don't stop looking at it until you have seen some of these profundities—or what Thomas Carlisle described in another connection, 'infinities and immensities' —in this glorious cross.

So I repeat the question. Why, why this? Why did this happen? Why did it ever happen, that the Son of God, the Prince of Glory, died? Let us look at the answer. We have it all here in the Scriptures. I am not going to draw on my imagination. I am not inventing any answers. You know, my friends, the more you know your Bible, the easier preaching becomes. I pity the poor man who is in difficulties about what to preach, Sunday after Sunday, hoping that something striking will happen in the news so that he can preach a topical sermon. All I have to do is to hold before you what the Scriptures tell us about this great event, because I know nothing apart from what I find here. I am as ignorant as everybody else about these matters. If I had not got the Scriptures I could not preach. I simply hold before you what the Scriptures themselves say. What, then, do they tell us? Why is the Son of God there on the cross?

The first thing they say is that it is not merely the action of men. Oh, but you say, it is men who are hammering in those nails. I agree, but that would be the remark of a very superficial observer. What made the men do it? Is there nothing behind them? You see the whole trouble in the world today is that we are all looking at everything superficially. We choose some activity, then we set up a royal commission to look into it, and we have a little superficial reporting. It makes no difference, nothing is any different, because we are superficial in our diagnosis, we are not able to see the depths of things beneath the surface. It is the same here.

Why do I say that it was not merely the action of men?

Why am I repeating that it was not merely an accident? My answer is, of course, that it was something that had been prophesied. Take the passage in Isaiah 53. It is an exact prophecy of what happened on the cross. Again, read the 22nd Psalm. That is another perfect prophecy of the death of our Lord upon the cross. It is prophesied many times in the Old Testament. Indeed, you will see it if you go back to books like Leviticus and other books of the law which people say they find utterly boring and beyond their understanding. If you only know how to read them, you will find that they are all pointing to the cross. Or go back to Exodus and the story of the exodus of the Children of Israel from the captivity of Egypt. Why did they have to kill that lamb, the paschal lamb, as we call it, at night and put its blood on the door posts and the lintels? It is just a prophecy of this. Everything in the Passover story points to this event.

There, then, is a great factor. Isaiah 53 puts it so plainly '... led as a lamb to the slaughter, and as a sheep ...'. It is all there. The Lord was not taken by surprise. It was all prophesied long ago. But, of course, we are not dependent upon the prophecies of the Old Testament only. Our Lord himself made certain very specific statements about this. In his conversation with that great man Nicodemus, recorded in John 3, he put it like this. He said that as the serpent was lifted up in the wilderness, 'even so must the Son of man be lifted up: that whosoever believeth in him should not perish, but have eternal life'. Now here is a prophecy of his death upon the cross, quite early on in his ministry. He reminded Nicodemus of the old story in the history of the people, the Children of Israel. In the wilderness snakes began to bite people and they were killed as the result. And the cure was this. A brazen serpent was fastened to a pole and lifted up and everybody who looked at the brazen serpent was healed (Num 21:9). That was a prophecy of me, said our Lord, 'As

66

Moses lifted up the serpent in the wilderness, even so must the Son of man be lifted up' (Jn 3:14). He was not taken by surprise when they took him and crucified him. He told his followers that it was coming. He went on repeating this. This New Testament prophecy, too, is a vital part of this message.

We read in John 12 of an end coming to his earthly ministry. Suddenly it comes to the end, as it were, and he is ready. The hour, he says, is come. *The hour.* What is he talking about? He is talking about his death. In a short time, he says, 'And I, if I be lifted up from the earth, will draw all men unto me' (Jn 12:32). You remember the context? Some Greeks had come along and they had approached some of our Lord's disciples. They said, 'We would see Jesus.' We would like to have a word with him, and talk with this new teacher. We have been hearing about him, and we want to know what he has got to say. It was probably a kind of intellectual curiosity and also a more general kind of curiosity in a wonderful teacher that had just appeared. And our Lord would not see them. He sent back a message saying that he could not see them, and he explains it by saying that so far he was only sent to the Jews, 'but when I am lifted up ...'. And in his account John comments, 'This he said, signifying what death he should die' (v.33). When I am lifted up, he says, then I will draw all men unto me, which means, not every single individual that has ever lived, but men of all nations, not only Jews but Greeks and anybody else. 'All men', men from all nations, I will draw unto myself. When I die, I shall be a universal saviour in that sense. He knew it was coming, and he repeated that on many other occasions. Take the one when he turned to his disciples after they had been asking for certain privileges. He replied, 'Now, I have a baptism to be baptized with; and how am I straitened until it be accomplished!' (Lk 12:50). He is again referring to his death.

Well there is evidence, and I could give you more, showing that this is no accident, no mere action on the part of
men. There is something more here. There is a mystery.
There is something behind it. The apostle Peter says the
same thing. On the day of Pentecost at Jerusalem, after the
Holy Spirit had come down upon the infant church, people
came together from all directions, astonished and amazed
because they heard these simple, unlettered men talking in
languages which they could understand. Every man heard
them telling in his own language the wonderful works of
God. And they were amazed and said, 'What is this?' and
thought they were drunk. With this Peter began to preach,
and he gave them the answer. He told them that this was
something that had been done to them by Jesus of Nazareth.
This is the first sermon really preached under the auspices
of the Christian church, and here therefore is the full explanation.

Peter then goes on to say to them: 'Ye men of Israel, hear
these words; Jesus of Nazareth, a man approved of God
among you by miracles and wonders and signs, which God
did by him in the midst of you, as ye yourselves also know:'
—take note—'him, being delivered by the determinate
counsel and fore-knowledge of God, ye have taken, and by
wicked hands [which can be better translated 'by the hands
of wicked men', because the Jews had used the Romans to
do it] have crucified and slain . . .' But you notice what Peter
says: Him, Jesus of Nazareth, Jesus Christ, him, 'being delivered by the determinate counsel and fore-knowledge of
God, ye have taken, and by wicked hands have crucified and
slain.' Yes, says Peter, it was your hands that did it. But it was
God who determined it. And God determined it not now,
but before time: in the pre-determinate counsel and fore-
knowledge of God. This is something, he says, that God
determined in eternity which you have actually done with

your own hands now in time.

Now, this is so important that it was repeated on another occasion. In Acts 4 we find a wonderful prayer meeting being held by the early Christian church. Two of their company, Peter and John, had been arrested, put on trial, and then forbidden to do any further preaching or teaching in the name of this Jesus. The authorities had said to them in effect, Look here, we are letting you off this time, but if you go on doing this, well then we will not only arrest you, but we will deal with you. And they were threatening them with death. They straightly charged them that they should do no more of this preaching in the name of Jesus. And then we find the apostles going back to their own company, to the church, where they all begin to pray, and this is what they say in that prayer. Having quoted the second Psalm, they say, '. . . For of a truth against thy holy child Jesus, whom thou hast anointed, both Herod, and Pontius Pilate, with the Gentiles, and the people of Israel, were gathered together, for to do whatsoever thy hand and thy counsel determined before to be done' (Acts 4:27–28). They are repeating what Peter had said in his sermon on the day of Pentecost, and what is said on both occasions is that though it was actually, of course, physically, materially, the hands of men who had killed him, it was God who had purposed this. They were simply carrying out in time what God had predetermined before the very foundation of the world.

Now, this is the most important thing that you and I can ever consider. You see what it means, and the light this throws upon all those burnt offerings and sacrifices in the Old Testament. As we saw, the paschal lamb and all the burnt offerings and sacrifices were just prophecies of the coming of the day when the Son of God was going to be crucified. Now you see how all that could happen. God had decided on this before man was ever created. He knew, he had decided before time, that this was to be the way in which man should be saved. God, you see, is omniscient. God knows everything, he knows the end from the beginning. There is nothing outside his knowledge. And God knew that man was going to fall before he made him, and God had decided upon a plan of salvation before man was ever created.

Now this is the whole of the preaching of the New Testament. The apostle Paul in writing to the Corinthians puts it like this: he says he has a wisdom to preach, 'Howbeit we speak wisdom among them that are perfect: yet not the wisdom of this world, nor of the princes of this world, that come to nought: but,' he says, 'we speak the wisdom of God in a mystery, even the hidden wisdom, which God ordained before the world unto our glory' (1 Cor 2:6–7). That is the very thing that I am trying to put before you. It means the most glorious good news that has ever come into the world. This is why the apostle Paul glories in the cross of Christ. Here we are, miserable sinners, every one of us. There is not a person alive today who is not a miserable sinner. The whole of the human race is in this condition. Everybody who has ever been born since the fall of Adam has been born in sin, shapen in iniquity. Life has been a misery for that reason. Life has been a trial. Life is a matter of disappointment. Life is a matter of a man doing things he does not want to do, and failing to do the things he wants to do. It is a struggle. It is a moral problem, a moral failure, and a moral difficulty to every one of us.

And here we are still in the same condition. Civilization has been trying to put things right. Men have concocted their schemes, planned their Utopias, and passed their acts of parliament and we are none the better. We are as bad as we have ever been, more educated, but not more moral. We know much that our forefathers did not, but we still do not know how not to sin, and how to live a clean, a wholesome, pure and a chaste life. Here we are in the same old human predicament. And do you know the message of this gospel? Do you know why Paul gloried in it? It is because he had come to see that God had got a plan for this miserable, wretched, failing sinful world. And it is a plan that he had planned before the very foundation of the world itself.

I know of nothing so wonderful in the whole world to-day. That is why I do not preach topical sermons, I have something to tell you that is worth listening to! What good are my comments upon the news, or upon politics? Everything goes round in the same old miserable way. I am here to tell you something that only this gospel can tell you. That the Almighty and Everlasting God is concerned about this, it is *his* world and he is going to put it right, and he is putting it right in his own way. He is concerned about our deliverance and about our redemption. God has a plan and a purpose: 'Him, being delivered by the determinate counsel and fore-knowledge of God, ye have taken, and by wicked hands have crucified and slain.' But you did not know what you were doing. You did not realize that this was a part of God's great and eternal plan and purpose of salvation and of redemption. The cross, you see, is the centre of God's plan. It is the heart of God's way of saving the world. That is why, as we have seen, the Apostle put it again in 1 Corinthians 1: 'But we preach Christ crucified, unto the Jews a stumbling-block, and unto the Greeks foolishness; but unto them which are called ... Christ the power of God, and the wisdom of God.' Here it is in its essence, this cross of Christ. That is why I want to put it to you like this. That the Apostle gloried in the cross, and every true Christian glories in it, because it is the greatest display and exposition of the character of the everlasting God. That is what you see when you survey the cross. You do not see that glorious person alone; you look again and see that it is not only the Son that is involved in this cross. The Father is involved, he is there. Have you ever seen him there? Is there anything higher or more wonderful than to see something of the glory of the everlasting God? It is on the cross on Calvary's hill that you see the most wonderful and amazing display of this glory that the world has ever known.

All our troubles ultimately emanate from our ignorance of God. That is the real trouble in the world today. Men and women do not know God. There are some who say they are not interested. There are others, and this is equally bad, who simply put up their own ideas of God. The men who speculate philosophically about God, these are the popular writers of today. They have no authority whatsoever. It is simply what they think. That is sheer ignorance of God. No, we cannot know God unless he reveals himself to us, because God is who and what he is. And what do we know? Do we know ourselves? Does your psychology really explain you to yourself? Does all your modern knowledge really help you to know yourself and your neighbour? Does it really give you an understanding of life and of death? Of course it does not! Our ignorance is appalling, and the more we learn, the more we see our own ignorance. How can a man know God?

> Immortal, invisible, God only wise,
> In light inaccessible hid from our eyes.
>
> W. Chalmers Smith

What is the use of Jodrell Bank when you are looking into infinity and eternity? By all means, send up your astronauts. Let them look with all the power that they can command; they cannot possibly see him. God is:

> Immortal, invisible, God only wise,
> In light inaccessible hid from our eyes,

> Most blessed, most glorious, the Ancient of Days,
> Pavilioned in splendour and girded with praise.

Do you think you can see? Of course you cannot. We are incapacitated at the very beginning, before we make any attempt. We see parts and portions.

In creation you can see something of him. As the Apostle puts it in Romans 1, by examining nature and creation, you can see something of the Creator's eternal power, and Godhead. You see, as it were, the marks of his fingers, and you know that God is, as Sir James Jeans put it, the great scientist, the mastermind and mathematician. You see it in the symmetry and the balance, and all the form and the perfection in the universe. You see it in the seasons, spring, summer, autumn, winter, and in his gifts to man, and all his kindness and goodness. Yes, but you only see in part, you only see God's power, God's greatness, God the Creator.

And then you can see some part of him in history. Read the history of the nations, and especially of the Jews. You see something of the hand of God, as the Lord of history. Again, you see it also in providence, in his providential dealings with us. But even when you have seen all these things, you have seen so little about God. You see that there is great power, great ability, and a great order. But, oh! You do not know God as a Father, you do not know God in his heart, you do not know God in all the glory of his fullness. John has put it perfectly to us in the prologue of his Gospel when he says, 'No man hath seen God at any time; the only begotten Son, which is in the bosom of the Father, *he* hath declared him' (1:18, italic mine). No man hath seen God; no man can see God and live. God being what he is, it is impossible. We can know nothing except it be revealed and this is the message of this Gospel, that God, in his infinite grace and kindness, has revealed himself, not only in nature and creation,

73

not only in providence and in history, but beyond it all, in his Son, who came from the eternal bosom to teach us about him and to tell us about him, and that supremely on the cross. That is why it is so glorious. Everything is leading up to this. There are hints and suggestions all the way, but here it bursts upon us in all the blaze of everlasting glory; God really revealing his heart to us.

Our Lord himself had said that this was the case. He said, 'I am the way, the truth, and the life: no man cometh unto the Father [which means no man *can* come unto the Father] but by me' (Jn 14:6). Yes, God the Creator, God the Almighty, God the Controller of history, but you will never know God as Father except by Jesus Christ, and in particular, by his death upon the cross. If you want to know God, if you want to know the everlasting and eternal God, this is the way, the only way. Look there, gaze, meditate, survey, the wondrous cross. And then you will see something of him.

The first thing you will see is the *grace* of God. Grace is a great word in the Bible, the grace of God. It is most simply defined in these words—it is favour shown to people who do not deserve any favour at all. And the message of the gospel is that any one of us is saved and put right for eternity, solely and entirely by the grace of God, not by ourselves. 'By grace are ye saved through faith; and that not of yourselves: it is the gift of God' (Eph 2:8). My friend, is it not about time we all admitted it? Do what you like, you will never save yourself. You will never save yourself from the world, the flesh, and the devil, you will never save yourself from your own misery. Still less will you save yourself from the law of God and judgement and hell. You cannot do it. Try! Men have tried it throughout the centuries. They have all admitted failure.

> Not the labours of my hands
> Can fulfil thy law's demands;

74

Could my zeal no respite know,
Could my tears for ever flow,
All for sin could not atone;
Thou must save, and thou alone.

A. M. Toplady

And the best and the most honest souls the world has ever known have been the ones that have tried that route most assiduously, and have been most ready at the end to confess their failure. No, there is only one hope for us today. It is the grace of God, which means that in spite of our being what we are, 'God so loved the world that he gave his only begotten son . . .'. He did it in spite of us. We deserve nothing but hell. If you think you deserve heaven, take it from me you are not a Christian.

Now, that is a very good definition of a Christian. Any man who thinks that he deserves heaven is not a Christian. But for any man who knows that he deserves hell, there is hope. Out goes all your self-righteousness. It is all by grace, and entirely the mercy and compassion and the grace of God. It is God, who, in spite of us, and, in spite of the world being what it is, sent his own Son into this world and then sent him to the cross. By the predeterminate counsel and fore-knowledge of God, he went there. Why? Here is the question. All right, you say, I like this idea of grace. I am glad to hear you saying that God still loves us in spite of our unworthiness and sinfulness. That is wonderful. But why the cross, then? Why does God in his love not just forgive us?

Look again at the cross, my friend. Take another survey. Examine it again with greater depth and profundity, and having seen the grace and the mercy and the compassion and the kindness of God, look again and this is what you will see. You will see the *righteousness* of God. You will see the justice of God and his holiness. It is the place of all places in the universe where these attributes of God can be seen most

75

plainly. God has revealed something of his righteousness, and his justice and his holiness, in the law that he gave to the Children of Israel. The Ten Commandments proclaim it and his punishments of the Children of Israel display the same thing.

But if you really want to know anything about righteousness and justice and utter, absolute holiness, you will have to survey the wondrous cross, and there you will see it, for what the cross tells us is that God hates sin. God is the eternal antithesis to sin. God abominates sin with the whole intensity of his divine and perfect and holy nature. And God not only hates sin, he cannot tolerate it. God cannot compromise with sin. That is what we want, of course. We want God to compromise with sin. We want a God who says: 'All right, I know you have done this or that, but it is all right. Slip into heaven.' God cannot do that. God cannot compromise. There is no compromise between light and darkness, good and evil. They are eternal opposites, and God, because he is God hates sin.

God must therefore punish sin. That is what the Bible means when it tells us that the wrath of God is against all sin and unrighteousness. 'For the wrath of God,' says the apostle Paul in his letter to the Romans, 'is revealed from heaven against all ungodliness and unrighteousness of men, who hold the truth in unrighteousness' (1:18). My friend, God is holy. Who can imagine this? We are so imperfect, so impure. Our minds are so polluted. You and I cannot think of absolute purity, absolute righteousness, absolute holiness. We may talk about these things, but we cannot imagine them. But God is all that. And because he is all that, he can have no dealings with sin. He has told us that he must and will punish the sinner because sin is what it is. Sin is rebellion against God. Do not think of sin merely in terms of actions. That is what we are all tending to do at the present time.

THE WISDOM OF GOD

The newspapers are placarding certain actions in their mock self-righteousness. But that is not what is meant by sin. Sin is a matter of attitude. And what makes sin sin, is that it is rebellion against God. It is to disobey God; it is to trample upon the sanctities of God. It is unrighteousness; it is transgression of God's law. Indeed, it is worse. It is a hatred of God.

The natural mind is not merely a mind that makes a man do things that he should not do. 'The carnal [natural] mind is enmity against God: for it is not subject to the law of God, neither indeed can be' (Rom 8:7). And it is because man in sin is such, that he regards even the gospel as foolishness. 'But the natural man receiveth not the things of the Spirit of God: for they are foolishness unto him: neither can he know them, because they are spiritually discerned' (1 Cor 2:14). This is sin, this is the trouble with man, that he is so steeped in sin and so perverted by it that when God does the most glorious thing that even God can do, the natural man laughs at it as foolishness and dismisses it with derision. That is why God hates sin. It is because it hates him. It is enmity against God. 'The carnal mind is not subject to the law of God, neither indeed can be . . . .'

Now the cross tells us that. And you see that because of that, the cross is necessary. Here is the problem. How can such a God possibly forgive any man, how can there be any hope of heaven for any one of us, for we have all sinned? We are all 'by nature the children of wrath,' says Paul to the Ephesians, 'even as others' (Eph 2:8). We are all naturally God-haters, and if you have not realized that, you have not known these things very deeply. Do not come and tell me that you have always loved God. You have not. You were born in sin, shapen in iniquity. And if you think you have always believed in God, it is because you have had a God of your own creation, not the God of the Bible. This is a universal statement, and so we have the problem. How can this holy, righteous God possibly forgive anybody at all, and remain what he is?

What I see in the cross is God's way of solving the problem. So I see the *wisdom* of God. If you want to know anything about the wisdom of God, look at the cross. Here is God's solution to the problem that he saw before he created the world. Man was going to sin, and yet God wants to forgive him. How can he? God, in his eternal wisdom, thought out the way and the plan.

> O loving wisdom of our God!
>   When all was sin and shame,
> A second Adam to the fight
>   And to the rescue came.

J. H. Newman

If you want to know anything about the eternal wisdom of God, look at the cross. That is why Paul says it is the wisdom of God and the power of God. There you see the mind of the eternal, solving the eternal problem. How can God be just and at the same time forgive anybody? How can he bring these things together—righteousness and mercy, holiness and love? Is it possible? And the answer is on the cross. This is why Paul glories in it. He has seen things there that he has never seen anywhere else. He was a wonderful Pharisee, a very good man, moral and religious. He studied the Scriptures, he thought he knew all about God, but here he discovers that he knows nothing. All his knowledge has become nothing to him. It is here that he sees the wisdom of God, providing a way, making a way, whereby God can remain God and yet forgive a sinner.

So you see there the wisdom of God, as well as his grace, and purpose, his mercy and his compassion. But I see another thing. I see the *immutability* of God, which means that Goes does not and cannot change. You see, the God of these moderns is a god not worth worshipping. He is a god who changes and accommodates, and no one can tell what he is going to do next. He changes every century, according to scientific knowledge and philosophical speculation. That is not God. God, said the fathers of the Bible, is immutable; he is unchangeable. He cannot deny himself. He is what he says he is. And if there is one place in all history and in the whole of the universe where you see the immutability and the unchangeableness of God more clearly than anywhere else, it is on the cross. Suffering there is his own Son. Is he going to change, is he going to modify? No, he sees what must be done, and he does it. God says that he is going to punish sin. And when even his own Son makes himself the representative of sinners, he carries out his word. He does not modify it, even though it is his own Son. Oh, the immutability of God, and the absolute perfection of all his ways!

But that leads me to the last thing, the most wonderful thing of all, which is the *love* of God to us. It is not surprising that this Apostle should say to the Romans, 'God commendeth his love toward us, in that, while we were yet sinners, Christ died for us' (Rom 5:8). How do you see the love of God in the cross? Ah, says the modern man, I see it in this way, that though man rejected and murdered the Son of God, God in his love still says, 'All right, I still forgive you. Though you have done that to my Son, I still forgive you.' Yes, that is a part of it, but it is the smallest part of it. That is not the real love of God. I have reminded you already that God was not a passive spectator of the death of his Son. That is how the moderns put it. That God in heaven looked on and down upon it all, he saw men killing his own Son, and he said, 'All right, I will still forgive you.' But in that view, God was passive, God was inactive. He was responding passively to what men did. Oh, how important we think we are. You know it is not we who brought his Son to the cross. It was God. It was the predeterminate counsel and foreknowledge of God.

If you really want to know what the love of God means, read what Paul wrote to the Romans, 'For what the law could not do, in that it was weak through the flesh, God sending his own Son in the likeness of sinful flesh, and for sin, condemned sin in the flesh' (Rom 8:3). God condemned sin in the flesh of his own Son. This is the love of God. Read again Isaiah 53, that wonderful prophecy of what happened on Calvary's hill. You notice how he goes on repeating it. 'Surely he hath borne our griefs, and carried our sorrows: yet we did esteem him stricken, smitten of God, and afflicted .... It pleased the Lord to bruise him; he hath put him to grief' (vv. 4, 10). These are the terms. And they are nothing but a plain, simple, accurate, factual description of what happened on the cross. Read Paul summing it all up: 'For he [God] hath made him [the Son] to be sin for us' (2 Cor 5:21). Do you realize what I am saying? Men and women, this is the whole trouble of the world. It is bound in its blindness. God has made his own Son to be sin for us, though he knew no sin, in order that he might be able to forgive us, in order 'that we might be made the righteousness of God in him'.

What does that mean? Let me give you another quotation from this apostle Paul who in Romans 8:32 describes why he glories so much in the cross: 'He [God] that spared not his own Son, but delivered him up for us all.' Now that is a wonderful description of what happened on the cross. God, in his great love to us, delivered up for us his only begotten, dearly beloved Son, who had never disobeyed him and had never done any harm to anybody, to the death of the cross. But you notice what he says: 'He that spared not his own Son.' He means that God had made it very plain and clear that he was going to punish sin by pouring out upon sinners the vials of his wrath. He was going to punish sin in this way—that men should die. The wages of sin is death, and it means endless death and destruction. And what we are told there by the Apostle is that after he had laid our sins upon his own Son on that cross, he did not spare him any of the punishment. He did not say, Because he is my Son I will modify the punishment. I will hold back a little, I cannot do that to my own Son. I cannot regard him as a sinner. I cannot smite him, I cannot strike him. He did not say that. He did everything he had said he would do. He did not keep anything back. He spared not his own Son. He poured out all his divine wrath upon sin, upon his own dearly beloved Son.

So you hear the Son crying out in his agony, 'My God, my God, why hast thou forsaken me?' and he literally died of a broken heart. John tells us that when the soldiers pierced his side with a spear, 'Forthwith came there out blood and water' (19:34). The heart had burst and the blood had clotted, and there it was—serum and blood clot, because his heart was literally ruptured by the agony of the wrath of God upon him, and by the separation from the face of his Father. That is the love of God. That, my friend, is the love of God to you, a sinner. Not that he looks on passively and says: I forgive you though you have done this to my Son. No, he himself smites the Son. He does to the Son what you and I could never do. He pours out his eternal wrath upon him, and hides his face from him. His own dearly beloved, only begotten Son. And he did it in order that we should not receive that punishment and go to hell and spend there an eternity in misery, torment and unhappiness. That is the love of God. And that is the wonder and the marvel and the glory of the cross, God punishing his own Son, in order that he might not have to punish you and me.

It was also done in order that the message of the cross might be preached, and it is this: 'Believe on the Lord Jesus

Christ, and thou shalt be saved' (Acts 16:31). Believe that he died your death, bore your punishment, suffered in your place, that the chastisement of your peace was upon him. Believe, and you are immediately forgiven. That is the glory of the cross. God's wisdom devising the way, God's love carrying it out, in spite of what it meant to him, and the Son, willingly and readily submitting himself to it, in order that you and I might be forgiven and might become the children of God. Oh:

> When I survey the wondrous Cross,
> On which the Prince of glory died,

—for he was put to death by his own Father—

> My richest gain I count but loss,
> And pour contempt on all my pride.

—and on all my self-righteousness. It is 'When I survey the wondrous cross' that I see these things: God eternal, in all the glory of his Father's heart, giving his own Son up to such a death for me.

And indeed I therefore see in that cross the harmony of all the divine attributes. I see holiness and love, I see 'Mercy and truth met together. Righteousness and peace have kissed each other.' I see all the eternal attributes of the everlasting God, all of them displayed at the same time. There is no contradiction between the righteousness, the justice and the love and the mercy and the compassion. They are all there, and they are all there in the plenitude of the Godhead. There is only one thing to say when you have seen things like that, and it is this: 'God forbid that I should glory, save in the cross of our Lord Jesus Christ.' It is there I know God as he is, and as my Father. And I see his glorious character vindicated to the last iota. Therefore I trust my soul to him. I rest upon his word, the unchanging, everlasting God.

Do you react like that to the cross, my friend? Have you seen these things in the cross—the Son, with the Father and the Holy Spirit sustaining the Son? He offered himself through the eternal Spirit on our behalf to God. It is your reaction to this that decides whether you are a Christian or not. Do not tell me about your good works, I am not interested. Do not tell me you are a church member, I am not a bit interested. Are you glorying in the cross? Is this everything to you? Is this life to you? Are you ready to die rather than deny this glorious message? That is what a Christian is, and unless we glory in the cross we have not seen it and what it means, and if we have not seen it, we do not really believe in it. And if we do not believe in it, we are yet in our sins, and should we die like that, we will go to judgement and we will go to hell. Your eternal, everlasting destiny, depends upon this one thing. Have you seen that God has provided there the only way whereby you can be forgiven and become a child of God, and go on to inherit the glories of eternity? May God have mercy upon us all, and by his Spirit open our eyes to see the glory of the cross.

Chapter 4

'Love Not the World'

'But God forbid that I should glory, save in the cross of our Lord Jesus Christ, by whom the world is crucified unto me, and I unto the world.'

As we continue in our consideration of this text, let me remind you that there was a time when Paul used to boast of something very different from the cross of Christ. He used to boast of the fact that he was an Israelite, an Hebrew of the Hebrews, of the tribe of Benjamin, circumcised on the eighth day—a man who was an expert in his knowledge of the law, a highly religious man, and so on. Those things used to be his boast and he was very proud of them. He was an intense man, a passionate man always, this apostle Paul. And he always let it be known what it was that he really believed in and what he made his boast in. That is how he once used to be. But what he is telling us here now is that all that has finished. 'God forbid that I should glory, save in the cross of our Lord Jesus Christ.'

And so the most appropriate question for us to consider now is what are we boasting about, what are we proud of? That tells us exactly where we all stand. We have already been able to see that the differentiating mark of the Christian is that he is a man who centres his whole thinking and makes his boast about, and is moved most deeply by, the cross of the Lord Jesus Christ. That is what tells us whether we are Christians or not.

Now, there are many people who think they are Christians when they are not. That is not my opinion, the Bible says it, and we know that it has been true throughout the centuries. There are people who think they are Christians simply because they are born in a particular country, or for other reasons of that kind. But *this* is the test—what is your boast? If you boast more in your country than in the cross of Christ, there is no need to argue about it, you are not a Christian. Does that sound drastic? That is Christian teaching. The apostle Paul used to boast of the fact that he was a Hebrew. He did not afterwards. He was still glad that he was. He does not derogate from his appreciation of being a member of the family of God's children on earth, even in a physical sense. But he does not boast of it. It must not be the big thing, the thing that moves us most of all. It must not come first.

This, then, comes to us as a very thorough test. The Christian is a man who makes his boast, who glories in, the cross of our Lord Jesus Christ, and we have considered a number of reasons for this. He does so because he knows that it is by the cross that he is saved. By, or through whom, we read here, 'the world is crucified unto me, and I unto the world'. It is the death upon the cross that saves us. And we have considered what that meant.

Then we have seen that even if we regard the cross merely as a spectacle, it is incomparable. Comparisons are odious, I quite agree. And yet we must make them. The world is very fond of spectacles, and of great events. There are great moments in the national history of practically every country in the world. All countries have great heroes, men who have done remarkable deeds, and so on. And people like to remember these and to read about them, to look at them and to think about them. And to rejoice in them, too, and to make their boast in them. All I am saying is that when one sees something of the real meaning of what happened when the Lord Jesus Christ died on the cross, everything else loses significance. Indeed everything would pale into insignificance, if only we really did understand what it meant to the Son of God to die there in that terrible manner upon the cross. As Isaac Watts has reminded us, there is only one inevitable result: 'My richest gain I count but loss, and pour contempt on all my pride.'

Again, we have seen how the cross is a revelation of the character of the eternal God, how it shows us and displays to us the attributes of God: God's eternal wisdom; God's plan for this world and the whole cosmos; God's justice, righteousness, holiness. Yes, and thank God, his love, and mercy and compassion, his commiseration with us, and his long-suffering. But as we survey the wondrous cross, the moment we begin to see the perfection of the plan, and something of the way he devised the means whereby anyone could be saved; when we see all this, nothing can ever again stand before that in our estimation. It is a sheer impossibility.

But we must go further. The Apostle tells us also that he glories in the cross because of what it has done to him, and what it has done for him. 'God forbid that I should glory, save in the cross of our Lord Jesus Christ, *by whom the world is crucified unto me and I unto the world.*' Now here is a new aspect of the matter. He glories in it, because of what it does to him, and this is the thing that he singles out particularly. He says, I am glorying in this cross because that is the thing that has crucified the world unto me. To crucify means to kill, to put to death, to render inoperative. It is like the crucifixion of our Lord himself. He expired upon the cross, he gave up the ghost, he died and his body was taken down and buried. Now, Paul says, that same cross crucifies the world and kills it as far as he is concerned; it removes it.

But why does he glory in this particular fact? This is indeed a most vital matter for us. The world and all that it stands for is the main cause of the tragedies that have happened in the human history of the world. It is the world and everything that that represents that has produced the two world wars. It is the world that produces all our trials and troubles and tribulations. Now that is the essence of biblical teaching from the very beginning to the very end. It is the world itself that is responsible for its own condition, and Christian preaching must show us the cause of our troubles, because until we are clear about the cause we will not get a cure. The first thing we must do is to diagnose. All the talk and the writing come to nothing, because people never really understand why things are as they are. And the answer that is given here by the Apostle in this great statement is that he thanks God that the cross has delivered him from the world. Why? Because the world is the cause of all our troubles by nature. And that is the reason why any man should glory in anything that delivers him from it, and the only thing that does deliver him from it is the cross of our Lord Jesus Christ.

According to the teaching of the Bible there are only two kinds of people in this world. There are the people who glory in the cross and those who do not. But let me put that in a different way. There are only two types of people in the world: there are those who belong to the world and who are men of the world, and who glory in that fact, and there are those who glory in the fact that they are no longer of the world. Though they are still in it, they glory that they are only strangers and pilgrims, travellers and journeymen, passing through this world of time.

Now that is the fundamental proposition of the whole of the Bible. There is this great division of mankind, and any other divisions are quite irrelevant. It does not matter what the colour of your skin is, or what your native country is, or what your nationality is. It does not matter whether you are wealthy or poor, learned or ignorant, nothing matters but just this. Are you a man of the world or are you a man of God? It is one or the other. There was a fundamental division in the whole of the human race way back at the beginning. You see it in Chapter 4 of Genesis. You are either like Abel or you are like Cain. Cain is the man of the world; Abel is the man of God. And ever since there has been that great division. The Bible goes even further and says that every one of us, by nature, is born into this world as belonging to the world, as a man of the world. None of us are born Christians, none of us are born without sin. We are all born in sin, we are all 'shapen in iniquity'. We are all born the children of Adam, the fallen man, and therefore we are all born as children of the world.

Now there is a very striking statement of this in Psalm 17:14 where this term is actually used: 'From men which are thy hand, O Lord, from *men of the world,* which have their portion in this life, and whose belly thou fillest with thy hid treasure, they are full of children' (italics mine). He wants to be delivered from such men, from those men of the world, who have their portion in this life. Now by nature, we are all of that type and belong to that category. The whole of humanity fell in Adam, and so we are all born with this bias against God and towards the world. And what the Apostle tells us at this point is that he glories in the cross and he thanks God for it, because this is the thing that has taken him from the world where he was, and put him into an entirely new position. It has crucified the world unto him, and he in turn is crucified unto the world.

What then does the world mean? What does it mean to say that a man is a man of the world and not a man of God? This is the thing that you hear men boast of, is it not? They do not do it as much now, perhaps, as I remember them doing it years ago. Then it was more popular and more usual for people to go to places of worship, and the really up-to-date man then was the man who said, 'No, I never go near a place of worship now, I am a man of the world.' And he was proud of it. There are as many of them today, but of course there is nothing to boast about. It is more of an exception not to be a man of the world by now.

But what is the meaning of 'world' in this context? Let me refer you to 1 John 2:15: 'Love not the world, neither the things that are in the world. If any man love the world, the love of the Father is not in him.' Now, in order to explain this, let me put it in this way. It does not mean the material universe, of course, it means an outlook and a point of view. 'The world' in the Bible usually means that. Sometimes it does mean the actual physical universe round and about us, the material universe, and then the context makes it plain. But here it does not. The world means life, viewed and thought of and lived, apart from God, apart from the Father. 'If any man love the world, the love of the Father is not in him.' That gives us our definition. The world is that view of life and death, and of man and of time, and of everything else entirely apart from God and his revelation as given in the Bible. That is the world. The world is that collection of people who think about all these things entirely apart from God and without God.

You find that the Apostle included in this definition human thinking, so-called philosophy. It does not matter what form it takes. Whether it is abstract or whether it is scientific, it makes no difference. It includes all thinking about man and his problems, and about the world and the ultimate, and life and death and all these things—all thinking which does not include God and is not governed by God's revelation. That is the world. The Apostle says 'the world by wisdom knew not God' (1 Cor 1:21), which means that man by searching cannot find God, and he has not, he has tried to, but he cannot, it is impossible. Paul says, 'Where is the wise? where is the scribe? where is the disputer of this world?' Let him come forward and speak. Here he is contrasting a thinking which excludes God and his revelation, with a thinking that is based solely and entirely upon God's revelation, and supremely in our Lord Jesus Christ.

So that is what is meant by the world: the outlook, the thinking and then in turn, of course, the behaviour. That is entirely human, entirely earthly, and entirely belongs to time. The apostle Paul has a wonderful description of this in Ephesians 2 where he says 'And you hath he quickened, who were dead in trespasses and sins; Wherein in time past ye walked according to the course of this world, according to the prince of power of the air, the spirit that now worketh in the children of disobedience' (vv. 1–2). He says it is a life lived according to the course of this world. It is that outlook upon everything that is bound entirely by human thinking and human ability, and you can see that it covers a very wide range. There are these learned infidel philosophers. Yes, but they are men of the world, who belong to it. Then you come to the other extreme, and you get the kind of thinking that is determined by the television and the radio, and the cinema. Well, that is not strange, it belongs to the same category, that is a philosophy of life. They do not use these magical scientific terms, and they do not talk about the absolute, and things like that. But it is a philosophy of life. It has got its teaching, and its point of view. It says this is the way to live. That is quite as much a philosophy as the other one. And it equally belongs to the world. God does not enter into either.

Well there is our definition of the world, and I can sum it up by putting it like this. It is that outlook which puts man at the centre, and makes man the ultimate authority. It is the view which says there is nothing but this world. What we have now is all that we will have. That is the worldly outlook, the mind of the world. That is the mind that is controlling the masses of the people, that controls all who are not Christians. The position is that man is the centre, man with his ability and understanding, and everything revolves around him. The supernatural is entirely discarded. They do not believe in it. There is nothing supernatural, nothing miraculous, nothing which is spiritual. There is nothing apart from what we know, what we can understand, what we can grasp, what we do, what we decide, what we determine. That is what is meant by the world. It makes man the centre of the universe, and he is the first and the last word upon everything. Man is his own authority; there is nothing above and beyond man. And man's life is confined entirely and completely to this world of time. When a man dies that is the end, there is nothing beyond that.

But, 'God forbid that I should glory, save in the cross of our Lord Jesus Christ, by whom the world is crucified unto me . . . .' Paul is proud of the fact that he has been delivered from that way of thinking, and we will see why when we consider, secondly, the characteristics of that world. There is no difficulty in defining them, we have our definition there, in 1 John 2:16. 'For all that is in the world, the lust of the flesh, and the lust of the eyes, and the pride of life, is not of the Father, but is of the world.' We must look at this. People often think, do they not of the two world wars, and the terrible loss of life, and all the blood and the lust and the carnage, the horror and the misery and the unhappiness. But what is the cause of it? The answer of the Bible is not in individual guilty personalities, like Hitler or Stalin, it is in nobody, except the world itself. It is this outlook, it is this non-Christian view of everything, that is the cause of it. And that is why this is so tremendously important. What is its characteristic? It is characterized by lust.

What is lust? Lust is a strong desire, and what the Bible says everywhere about this worldly life is that it is a life that is controlled by desire. Oh, I know the clever people will not have this, they say that they are governed only by their intellects. But let us be practical, let us be honest, let us be frank with one another. What the non-Christian says is, 'It is one thing to talk, but what do you do?' All right, let us apply that to them too. They say they are living a life purely in the intellect. Are they? Well I think the answer is to be seen in the newspapers. It does not matter how great their brains are, they are governed by desire and by lust just as much as everybody else.

But what does this mean? It means what the psychologists call urges or drives. Man is a creature with tremendous urges in him. He has been made like that, he has these primitive instincts in him, and they are powerful, so when a man is a man of the world they are more powerful than his mind. I cannot believe that a sane man would deliberately get drunk, but men do get drunk. I cannot believe that a man really controlled by his brain would deliberately smash another man's marriage and cause intense misery to innocent little children. But people, even very clever people, do that sort of thing. That is lust. It is lust that makes them do it, it is passion, desire, it is these tremendous drives that are more powerful than all our reason. We know it is wrong and still we do it because we like these things—the lust, the inordinate affection. John classifies it as 'the lust of the flesh' and it means that this life of the world that is so opposite to the life of God, the life of the Father, is a life that lives mainly for the body. We need not stay with this. We all know all about it, and if we do not know about it in personal experience, we cannot evade it as we walk about the streets of our cities and look at the hoardings, and at the way people are living, and listen to what they are talking about.

What are people living for? They live to eat, and to drink. 'You are no man,' they say, 'if you do not drink.' And the television tells you that repeatedly. But does drinking make a man a man? To them, this is life. Drink, alcohol, stimulus, lust of the flesh, the body, eating and drinking. The fuss and the attention that is paid to all this. And then, of course, sex. This is a sex-ridden generation. It is a sex-ridden world. You cannot get away from it. It is everywhere, it is an obsession, and is governing people. It is everything. This is the great interest. Any lurid details in books or papers about people's personal lives, with all that they suggest—everybody buys them. This is the thing that sells. That is lust—lust of the flesh. This is the way of the world.

John wrote his letter 1900 years ago, but he might very well have written it yesterday. It is such a perfect description of the world still. This is life apart from God. We, of course, are twentieth century people, we are very clever, we have advanced a great deal compared with people who lived in the first century. But, if we are living exactly as they did, and think as they did, where is the difference. There is *none*. Man remains exactly what he has always been.

But then he speaks of the lust of the eyes also. What is this? Here we have a very subtle bit of analysis. This is very profound psychology—lust of the flesh—lust of the eyes. What is this? Ah, this is the worship of appearance, the show, the pomp. It is everything external as opposed to the heart. Our Lord turned on the Pharisees one afternoon and he said, 'Ye are they which justify yourselves before men; but God knoweth your heart: for that which is highly esteemed among men is abomination in the sight of God' (Lk 16:15).

The eyes, that which can be seen, the external, and of course the whole world, is living along this very line at the present time. What it really means is that it is sham, it is pretence, it is dishonest. Is this not one of the great characteristics of the whole of life today? There was a time when there was some meaning or sense in the term 'good looking'. There is not any more. What you see is the paint and the powder, the makeup. That is the lust of the eyes. It is not true, it is not honest. You do not see the natural colour of the hair, it has turned to something else. It is an appearance. It sounds trivial, does it not? But it is very profound, for this is the view of life. Everything to give an appearance. It does not correspond to the facts and to the reality. It is the paint and the powder, not the broken heart that is behind it: the appearance of your reality. It is dishonest. It is the lie that is being enacted.

Again, our Lord put it in terms of the Pharisees. He says, You keep clean and wash the outside of the cup and the platter, but inside—what do you find there? There you will see everything that is foul. The outside looks so wonderful, but you do not look inside. There you will see the dirt and the filth. It has not been cleaned. As long as it looks marvellous, that is all that matters. These are the things, the lust of the flesh, and the eyes. And then, to cap it all, the pride of life, and they all go together—cutting a great figure in this world, that is what matters. Ambition and pride, the desire to get on that is the pride of life. These are the things in which people boast, and for which they live, and in which they glory; the desire for applause, the desire to get on, the desire to see your name in the papers, or on posters outside some building. This is lust. This is pride of life, wanting to be great and important. And the whole world pursues it.

This is the biblical analysis of the worldly man and his life, this life which is lived apart from God, the kind of life which people today think is so clever. This is the thing for which they have left Christianity—the lust of the flesh and the lust of the eyes, and the pride of life. I am working through this analysis to bring you to this point. This is what makes it so terrible. It is not only that of itself it is unworthy, it is what it leads to. It is bad enough in and of itself, but it leads to lack of order, to lack of discipline. It leads to lawlessness, and to licence. That was the whole sin of Cain at the very beginning. He took the law into his own hands. He was annoyed with God. His brother had kept God's law which decreed that an offering to God must be a blood sacrifice. Cain had not done so. God pointed it out to him. He could have been forgiven, restored, if he could only have found a sin offering, but he did not, and he was annoyed. He rebelled. He took the law into his own hands, and murdered his brother.

And that is what the worldly outlook always leads to. Every man becomes his own authority and his defence is, Why shouldn't I? Is that not our great problem in this country today? Is that not why morality is breaking down round and about us? Why not, says the world, why shouldn't I? I couldn't care less. What does it matter what the Bible says? What does it matter what the mid Victorian says? What does it matter what the philosopher says? What does it matter what anybody says? I want to, so why shouldn't I? Taking the law into your own hands, that is lust. That is desire in control, that is complete lawlessness and utter indiscipline.

And, of course, this desire to gratify ourselves brings in its train ugly things like jealousy. We become jealous of somebody whose pride of life looks a bit better than ours, or who gets more admiration that we do. We feel the same of somebody who does better than we do in the same profession or in the same business, or who has a better car. It is the pride of life again. And people cannot sleep at night for jealousy and envy. This is life, this is the world. Did anyone think that

Christianity and its preaching was just a little bit of soft stuff, and that preaching was to tell pleasant little stories and that Christians sang nice hymns and did not face life? I am asking you to face life at this moment in a way that nothing else in the world asks you to do. Jealousy and envy, malice and spite and hatred; it does not stop at that. It leads to theft and robbery. This lust of the flesh, the desire for another man's wife—it is robbery. We punish people who steal property, we do not punish a man who steals another man's wife, or a wife who steals another woman's husband. That is the madness of our legal system. Of course, when Hitler marched into Austria in 1938, and annexed it to Germany, we held up our hands in horror. The rape of Austria, we called it. We walked in and he took it. We say nothing when a man does that in private, perhaps we even admire him. The world certainly seems to admire him. It regards that as entertainment. It seems that it is a form of entertainment to depict a drunken man, or to depict an adulterous man, a man who flirts with another man's wife, or who does anything he should not. God have mercy upon us!

But, you see, finally it leads to strife, and in the end it leads to war. When nations do this sort of thing—as they do—it leads to war. All wars are ultimately a strife between the haves and the have nots. Some big bully wants to take another piece of land. Other people say, It is ours, we do not want you to take it. And there is a war. And so it goes on. One big bully has got what he wants, but another big bully says, I want some of it, and there is a fight between the two big bullies. And there you have the whole of human history. The strong against the weak, and the strong against the strong. It is nothing but lust. It is this desire, this lawlessness, this greed, this aggression. This is the outcome of the worldly life, that is characterized by the lust of the flesh and the lust of the eyes, and the pride of life. The apostle James in his epistle put the question which we should do well to ponder: 'From whence come wars and fightings among you? come they not hence, even of your lusts that war in your members? Ye lust, and have not: ye kill, and desire to have, and cannot obtain: Ye fight and war, yet ye have not, because ye ask not' (Jas 4:1). There is the verdict of the Bible, and the whole of human history. And that is why the world is as it is today.

Now that is the world. That is what it is, that is what it leads to, that is how it expresses itself. But Paul says, 'God forbid that I should glory, save in the cross of our Lord Jesus Christ, by whom the world is crucified unto me, and I unto the world.' I have got nothing more to do with it. How does the cross crucify the world unto us? Let me give you some answers to the question. It does it first and foremost by showing us the world for what it really is. There is nothing that shows us the real nature and character of the world except this book which I am expounding to you. And you find this supremely in the Lord Jesus Christ himself. The Lord Jesus Christ is the eternal Son of God, but he came into this world. Why did he ever come into it? Have you ever pondered that question? There is only one answer. Because the world is as I have been describing it to you. That is the only answer. The world is so violent, so rotten, that nothing can save it but the coming of the Son of God. That is why he came, and his very coming opens our eyes to the state of the world. Apart from him people say: 'Oh no! Look here, this is too black a picture, you are a pessimist. My dear sir,' they say, 'things are not as bad as that, you know. No, these things can be put right.'

'How can they be put right?' I ask.

'Well,' they answer, 'the real trouble is that people are not sufficiently educated.'

And so they debate and dispute about how education can be improved. But however well educated people become, the problem will still be there. We have been doing that throughout the centuries, and it does not make the slightest difference. No, the very fact that the Son of God ever came into the world is a pronouncement that the world is hopeless. If anything could have saved this world, the law that God gave to the nation of Israel through Moses would have done it. But it did not. It completely failed. That is why the Son of God had to come. The law is the schoolmaster to bring us to Christ. It was never meant to save. It was not big enough to do so. 'What the law could not do, in that it was weak through the flesh, God sending his own Son in the likeness of sinful flesh and for sin, condemned sin in the flesh' (Rom 8:3). It is the only way. But listen, look at him when he did come into this world, look how different he was. The description of him in Isaiah 53 is 'he hath no form nor comeliness ... that we should desire him'. His visage is marred. There was nothing of the pride of life about his appearance, nothing to appeal to the lust of the eyes. And then he was meek and he was lowly. He was pure, he was clean, he was holy. He sacrificed himself. He gave himself, he served. Lord of Glory though he was, he washed people's feet. He rendered an utter and a perfect obedience to the holy law of God. And it says here, look at him. You see what the world is. You take your great men of the world, so called, in whom we all glory, and in whom we boast. Put them by him and there is nothing. He condemns them all. What puny creatures they are side by side with him.

But come, let us look at this further. If you want to know what this world is like, look what it did to him. There was the Son of God. He had left the throne of heaven, he had come and humbled himself, and he gave himself to healing people, and to instructing them. He never did anyone any harm. He went about doing good. What was the response of the world? It hated him, it persecuted him, it rejected him. It chose a murderer before him. It crucified him, it killed him. And there on the cross he exposed the world for what it is. And the clever men of the world today are laughing at the cross, they are mocking it, they are jeering at it, they are making fun of the blood of Christ, and they are trying to ridicule it. They are only doing what their prototypes did in the first century. That is what the world has always done to him.

But there is another aspect. His entire emphasis was the exact opposite of the emphasis of the world. The world emphasizes, as we have seen, the lust of the flesh, the lust of the eyes, and the pride of life. What did he emphasize? He emphasized something that the world never speaks about at all. He emphasized the soul.

'For what shall it profit a man,' he said, 'if he shall gain the whole world, and lose his own soul?' What if you are the most handsome man or woman the world has ever known, and are always dressed in a most gorgeous manner and what if you have the greatest palace to live in, and have the greatest collection of motor cars and everything else? What if you have the whole world, and lose your own soul? That is what he says about the world, and he says it supremely there upon the cross. 'Or what shall a man give in exchange for his soul?' (Mk 8:36, 37). Why did he die? He died for the souls of men, not for our material welfare, not to reform this world, but to save our souls. 'The Son of man is come to seek and to save that which was lost' (Lk 19:10). And it is the *soul* that is lost. The thing that the world knows nothing about, but it is in you, and in all of us—this imperishable thing in us that goes on beyond death and the end. No, he exposed the lie of this world for what it really is. He spoke a parable about Dives and Lazarus. The rich man in his palace, dressed gorgeously, in wonderful robes, eating with all his boon companions until he had his fill, while the poor beggar sat at the gate with the dogs licking his sores. Oh, the Lord says in effect, do not judge superficially, that is not the end of the story. He gives us a picture of Lazarus in Abraham's bosom, and Dives in the torment of hell. You can see the difference between the mind and the outlook of the world, and the mind and the outlook of the Father, and the Son of God. He exposes the world for what it is. The moment you meet Christ, you see the world as something that is your enemy, something tawdry. You see that it has got the principle of death in it. And you no longer live for it and you no longer boast of it.

> The boast of heraldry, the pomp of pow'r,
>   And all that beauty, all that wealth e'er gave,
> Awaits alike th' inevitable hour,
>   The paths of glory lead but to the grave.
>
> *Thomas Gray*

But wait a minute that is not the end. It is the end as the man of the world sees it, but it is not so, for our Lord on his cross shows us the fate of the world. Not only does he show us the character of the world, he also shows us the fate that is awaiting it. And that is why the Apostle glories in the cross. John says, 'Love not the world, neither the things that are in the world . . . . the lust of the flesh, and the lust of the eyes, and the pride of life . . . .' 'The world passeth away,' he says, 'and the lust thereof' (1 Jn 2:15–17). And it is passing away. Many things are passing away in this generation to which you and I belong. What a change any one of us who is over fifty years of age has seen during his or her lifetime. The world, and its glory, is dying as we look at it. 'Change and decay in all around I see.' But that is as nothing compared with what is finally going to happen to this world. For its end will be the judgement. 'The whole world lieth in wicked-ness' (1 Jn 5:19). Our Lord, just before the cross, said, 'Now is the judgment of this world: now shall the prince of this world be cast out' (Jn 12:31). This is the judgement of the world, he says, I am dying and as I die I am going to judge the world.

From beginning to end the message of the Bible, this revelation of God, is that there is to be an end to the world, and that the end is judgement. The Christ of God will come back into this world and he will return to judge it. Listen to what we are told is the favourite verse of most people: 'For God so loved the world, that he gave his only begotten Son, that whosoever believeth in him should not perish, but have everlasting life.' If you believe in him you will not perish, if you do not believe in him you will perish. That is the statement of John 3:16. The world is under judgement. And it is going to perish. All that is opposed to God is going to be judged and it is going to be destroyed. There is a day coming when this whole universe will be judged by the return of the Son of God. And all that does not belong to him, but to the world, is going to be destroyed everlastingly. There is a day coming when astonished humanity is going to hear this cry: 'Babylon is fallen, is fallen' (Rev 14:8). What is Babylon? It is the world without Christ. It is London without Christ. It is New York without Christ. It is all these modern infernos without Christ. Babylon the great, Babylon is fallen, is fallen. This Babylon which seemed so great and wonderful, with its palaces and its great businesses, transacted with all the kings and the princes, and the great of the earth, who all brought their merchandise to it. They boasted of it. How great, they said, is Babylon. That is the world without Christ. But the day is coming when he will judge it, and this Babylon will fall, it will be crushed to rubble and to nothing.

Christ on the cross says, 'Now is the judgment of this world.' He prophesies what is going to happen. He is to be the judge. '. . . he will judge the world in righteousness,' says the apostle Paul to the Athenians, 'by that man whom he hath ordained; whereof he hath given assurance unto all men, in that he hath raised him from the dead.' And Revelation 20:12–13 tells us that the books will be opened, and every man will have to stand before him, those who died at sea, those who died on land, those who were blown to nothing in the air, all will come back and stand before him in the final judgement.

And the simple message of the whole of the Bible is that the world, everything that is opposed to God and trusts in man and in his own power, is all going to be judged and condemned to everlasting misery and destruction. Now you see why Paul glories in the cross. It is the cross alone that saves any one of us from the destruction which is coming to the world. The whole world lieth guilty before God, 'For the wrath of God is revealed from heaven against all ungodliness and unrighteousness of men, who hold the truth in unrighteousness' (Rom 1:18). The whole world is going to be judged, and going to be destroyed. We are all born in the world and of it. And unless we can be separated from that world, we will share its fate. God forbid that I should glory, save in the cross of the Lord Jesus Christ, by which the world is crucified unto me, and I separated from it. How? Let me make it clear. On that cross, the Lord Jesus Christ took upon himself the punishment that is coming to all who belong to the world. That is why he died, he was receiving the punishment of the sins of men.

If then you believe in him, if you have seen all these things, and realize that there is only one way whereby you can be separated from the punishment of that world, that is by believing that Christ has borne the punishment for you, that he bore your sins in his own body on the tree, and that he has received your punishment, if you see all this, you are separated out of that world, so that when the destruction of the world comes, you are saved, and will not be involved in it. The cross of Christ separates all of us from the doom that is awaiting this evil world. It is the only thing that does. The punishment, as we have seen, must descend, and the punishment has descended upon him, and if I believe in him it will not descend on me. I no longer belong to the world, I belong to Christ, because he not only separates us *from* the world, he separates us *unto* himself and into his own kingdom.

What is a Christian? Paul tells the Colossians that a Christian is a man who has been translated from the kingdom of darkness into the kingdom of God's dear Son. I no longer belong to the world, I belong to the kingdom of Christ, the kingdom of light, the kingdom of glory, the kingdom of God. Here I am and the world has nothing to do with me. I am not of it. I am in this other kingdom. Oh, I am still existing in this world, but I no longer belong to it. I have been translated. And my citizenship is now in heaven, from whence also we look for the Saviour, and we know that we shall ever go on and be with the Lord. He, by dying on the cross, separates me from the world, puts me into his own kingdom, introduces me to God, and makes me a child of God, and an heir of eternal bliss.

So I come back and I look at the world, the world that used to fascinate me and entrance me, and make me think it was so wonderful, with its glittering prizes. I vied with others for them. I wanted them, and I thought how marvellous to be this or that. But, oh now, having seen him and this truth that he brings out, I look at them again, and I say,

> My richest gain I count but loss,
> And pour contempt on all my pride.

> *I. Watts*

He delivers me from the world. He died that, 'Whosoever

believeth in him should not perish, but have everlasting life.'
He does more, he gives me a power that is greater than the
world. Listen to John again: '. . . greater is he that is in you, than
he that is in the world', and, 'This is the victory that over-
cometh the world, even our faith', our faith in him (1 Jn 4:4, 5:4).

And, thank God, he does something else. He gives us
occasional glimpses of that other world, that real world, that
pure, that holy world, that is yet going to be. This old world
can never be improved and reformed. The whole of history
proves this. But when Christ comes back again to judge and
to destroy his enemies—all who belong to the world and
who have not got the love of the Father in them—he will set
up this new world: 'New heavens and a new earth, wherein
dwelleth righteousness' (2 Pet 3:13). A renovated cosmos, a
perfected universe, with glory everywhere. The glory of the
Lord shall cover everything as the waters cover the seas.
And if you believe in him and in his message, if you believe
that that person dying on that cross on Calvary's hill was the
Lord of Glory, and that he was dying in order to save you
and to separate you from the world, and to prepare you for
that glory, you will be in it and you will be glorying in it, and
spending your eternity with him in the glory.

And once a man sees this, as the apostle Paul had come to
see it, and as by the grace of God even I have come to see it,
this is what he says:

> Saviour, if of Sion's city
>   I, through grace, a member am,
> Let the world deride or pity,
>   I will glory in thy name:
> Fading is the worldling's pleasure,
>   All his boasted pomp and show;
> Solid joys and lasting treasure
>   None but Sion's children know.
>
> *J. Newton*

What are you glorying in? Are you glorying in this world still? There are only two possibilities. You either glory in the world in some shape or form, or else you glory in the cross of our Lord Jesus Christ, by which the world has been crucified unto you, and by which you are delivered from it in time, in order that you may share that everlasting glory with him.

Chapter 5

The Triumph of the Cross

'But God forbid that I should glory, save in the cross of our Lord Jesus Christ, by whom the world is crucified unto me and I unto the world.'

As we have been studying this great verse, we have seen that for the Christian, the cross is the most wonderful thing that has ever happened, and it is very important that we should be clear about this. Let me put it in this way. The Christian church, very rightly, has always referred to the day on which our Lord's death is commemorated as *Good* Friday. I remember a man coming to me once who said, 'You know, I cannot understand why you call this Good Friday.' And when I asked what we should call it, he said, 'You should call it Bad Friday. It was the day on which that terrible thing happened. Why do you call it Good Friday?' And thereby of course the poor man revealed to me that he had never really understood the meaning of the cross. He had never understood what happened there. A man who objects to calling it 'Good Friday' is one who is admitting that he has never gloried in the cross. It is Good Friday because of the wonderful thing that happened there. It is a good Friday because it was the Friday on which the Son of God did that without which none of us could ever be saved.

Without that, none of us could ever come to a knowledge of God.

Now, that is just another way of saying that we glory in it, in Good Friday, the best day that has ever happened in the history of the human race. I realize that the moment I say that, I am testing the view of everybody who is at this moment considering these words on the cross of the Lord Jesus Christ. If you do not end by seeing that it was good, glorious, wonderful, the best thing that has ever happened anywhere, you are misunderstanding it, and you are mis-interpreting it. But the Apostle glories in it. And we have seen something of why he does. And that is what we are going to continue doing now. It is the thing, he says, by which we are saved, delivered from our great enemy, the world. It is the thing in which one really sees fully the person and the glory of the Lord Jesus Christ. It is also the place, the act, in which one sees the glory of God the Father—the truth concerning the Father. And I am sure that the trouble with most of us is that we have never seen the greatness, the grandeur, and the extent of the cross.

So then, we must continue with this survey of the cross. It fulfils all the things we have been dealing with, but now I want to call attention to another aspect. We want to look at the cross now to see in it the way in which it delivers us from the power of the devil. I wonder how often you have thought of the cross like that? The cross is a great victory. It is the final move, as it were, here on earth in a great battle, a great conflict, a great crusade. I want to call your attention now, therefore, to the cross as it displays to us the Lord Jesus Christ as a victor, as a conqueror. We sometimes sing a hymn, 'Oh, Jesus, King most wonderful, thou conqueror re-nowned ....' I wonder how often we have considered it from that aspect? When you think of the cross what do you instinctively see there? What do you find? Do you find all these things there?

So, then, I want us to look at this aspect of the matter, and in this connection there is a passage in Colossians 2:15, where Paul put the matter very clearly. He writes, 'And having spoiled principalities and powers, he made a show of them openly, triumphing over them in it.' That is what was happening, he says, on the cross. He has been saying that what happened there was that the Lord blotted out 'the handwriting of ordinances that was against us [which was contrary to us] and took it out of the way, nailing it to his cross' (Col 2:14). We have considered that. 'And having spoiled principalities and powers, he made a show of them openly'—he has ridiculed them—'Triumphing over them in it'—through it or by it. The cross is a marvellous exposition of the triumph of the Son of God over the devil and all his forces and powers.

Let us look at it like this. This subject follows on very logically, and indeed quite inevitably, for those who believe the Bible, from the matter that we were considering earlier. The Apostle says that he glories in the cross because it is by the cross that the world has been crucified to him and he to the world, and we have seen what that meant. We have seen, too, that all our troubles in our personal lives, and in the whole life of the world today, are due to the fact that the world is what it is. This outlook, this way that man thinks apart from God, that is the cause of wars, it is the cause of every trouble. I think I have been able to prove that to you. Yes, but we cannot leave it at that; we are bound to ask another question. Why is the world as it is? Why should the world be like that? Now, that, I suggest to you, is one of the most profound questions that we can ever put. And it is the question that is always put by the Bible, for the Bible is the profoundest book in the world today. There are clever people who do not go to places of worship—that is true of about 90% of the people of this country. How do they spend their Sunday? Well, they have been reading the Sunday newspapers. I do not mean now necessarily the reports of the law courts or the police courts. I am thinking of the sophisticated, clever people who have been reading the articles—those by the great thinkers—and the reviews of the learned books on philosophy and history and various other matters. These men who, because of their learning and their knowledge, have long since given up considering Christianity. These men who are really concerned about doing something about this world and putting it right.

Now, all I have to say about them is that the trouble with all that is that it is so indescribably superficial. That is why it never comes to anything. That is why all civilization is not affected. That is why, in spite of all the effort of the centuries, we are in this terrible predicament as a world today. And the trouble is entirely due to the fact that these people have never really faced the problem of the condition of men and of the world in a profound manner. It is all so superficial. This is all most alarming, and it is still going on. Not a week passes but that we find that some new royal commission or some process of investigation is to be set up. They are going to tackle the problems, the juvenile delinquency and all these other things. But they have been doing it all before, this is nothing new. It is all because they have never asked the fundamental question. And the fundamental question is this: why is the condition what it is? Why is the world as it is? Why is there this worldly outlook? That is the profound question, and it is the question which, I claim, is raised and answered only by the Bible.

Let me put the answer before you. It is covered by this great biblical teaching about the devil and his forces and his powers. I cannot at this point take you through all the evidence, but I must point out some of the most important pieces found in the teaching of our Lord himself, in Luke 11:14: 'And he was casting out a devil, and it was dumb. And it came to pass, when the devil was gone out, the dumb spake; and the people wondered. But some of them said, He casteth out devils through Beelzebub the chief of the devils. And others, tempting him, sought of him a sign from heaven.' Now, this is our Lord's teaching. He says, 'But if I with the finger of God cast out devils, no doubt the kingdom of God is come upon you' (v.20). Then he adds: 'When a strong man armed keepeth his palace, his goods are in peace: But when a stronger than he shall come upon him, and overcome him, he taketh from him all his armour wherein he trusted, and divideth his spoils.' Now that is our Lord's own account of that he was doing in this world. The strong man armed, he says, keeps his palace, and when he does so, his goods are in peace. That is our Lord's way of describing this world, and life in it. Life in this world is like a great palace which is dominated by its keeper, this strong man armed. And 'his goods are in peace'. This means he is governing them, he is ruling them and he is controlling them. And they can do nothing at all about him. They cannot escape. 'But,' says the Lord, 'when a stronger than he shall come upon him'—that is his way of describing himself—'and overcome him, he taketh from him all his armour wherein he trusted, and divideth his spoils.' He will release these goods that were kept in peace, and set them at liberty. That is our Lord's own description of his work in this world. He has come to deal with this 'strong man armed' who is the devil, who keeps men and women in the thraldom of his own tyranny and power.

Let me also give you one or two more illustrations of the same teaching, as you find it in the teaching of the Apostles. I give you this evidence for one reason only—that I know that the average man in the world today, not only does not be-

lieve in the devil and his powers, but thinks this is the greatest joke of all. And indeed there are many in the church who
no longer believe in the devil. We have all become so clever,
and that is why the world is getting worse. We do not believe
in the existence of the one who really causes the whole
trouble. So read Paul in 2 Corinthians 4:3–4: 'But if our
gospel be hid, it is hid to them that are lost. In whom the
god of this world hath blinded the minds of them which
believe not, lest the light of the glorious gospel of Christ,
who is the image of God, should shine unto them.' The same
thing. The god of this world, blinding and keeping men in
the dark.

Then take another passage, from Ephesians 2:1: 'And you
hath he quickened, who were dead in trespasses and sins;
wherein in time past ye walked according to the course of
this world, according to the prince of the power of the air,
the spirit that now worketh in the children of disobedience.'

Listen to Paul in Ephesians 6:12: 'For we wrestle not
against flesh and blood, but against principalities, against
powers, against the rulers of the darkness of this world,
against spiritual wickedness in high places.'

And the teaching is not confined to the apostle Paul. All
these apostles repeated the teaching that was given to them
by their blessed Lord and Master, so the apostle John puts it
like this in 1 John 5:18–19: 'We know that whosoever is
born of God sinneth not; [does not go on sinning] but he
that is begotten of God keepeth himself, and that wicked
one toucheth him not. And we know that we are of God, and
the whole world lieth in wickedness.' And the word means
that the whole world lies in the embrace of the wicked one.
He has got them in his arms, he is embracing them and
holding them to himself. The whole world.

Now those are just specimens of biblical teaching. And
what I am trying to put to you is that this is the explanation

of why the world is as it is. Is it not about time we faced this question? Why are things as they are? Why have we had the two world wars? Ah, says somebody, the Kaiser, Mussolini, Hitler. Do you believe that? What made those men what they were? Even if they were mainly responsible what made them what they were? Is it merely men, are we merely wrestling against flesh and blood? What is the matter with the men and women of the present time? In view of all our advantages, all our education and so on, why is there all this moral muddle? Not only that, but why this almost incredible folly that is being put before us so regularly day by day? Why do people behave in such an utterly mad and unintelligent manner? Why can they be amused by the things by which they can be amused, with the world as it is today? What is the explanation?

The answer which the Bible gives is that it is not merely human nature. Man, I know, is a fool, we are all fools. But even that is not enough to explain the present state of the world, that of every individual human being. We are all conscious that there is something wrong, and we strive to be better. But we always fail. What is it that has dogged every human effort to improve the world, that vitiates all human effort? Why is it that, in spite of all the efforts of civilization after civilization, the world is as it is today? What is this thing that is dogging the fate of man, and ever holding him down? That is the question.

And the Bible has an answer to the question, the only answer. It is not man only, it is not human nature alone. We wrestle not against flesh and blood. We are not suffering merely from a kind of evolutionary lag. How much longer is the lag going to last? No, there is no evidence of this upward march. The world is as it has always been, in this terrible predicament that it is in today. No, it is not man. There is something behind man, something deeper. The biblical answer is that it is the devil. 'For we wrestle not against flesh and blood, but against principalities, against powers, against the rulers of the darkness of this world, against spiritual wickedness in high [in heavenly] places' (Eph 6:12).

Now, let me put this to you as concisely as I possibly can. According to the Bible, the whole trouble with the world was initiated by this one who is called the devil. You see, there is an unseen spiritual world. That is why the world goes wrong. It is not my purpose here to criticize statesmen, or philosophers, or anybody else, but it is simply a truism, that all their efforts are valueless and come to nothing, because they do not recognize the unseen spiritual realm. They always operate in the realm of the seen. They operate with human nature, and they make their investigations and they try to understand. They do not realize that there is something bigger than man. There is an unseen spiritual realm which is constantly influencing us, and, according to the Bible, it is a realm which can be divided into two main sections. There is God the Father, Son, and Holy Spirit. There is, on the other hand, the devil and all his forces and powers, the 'principalities and powers' and all that he governs and controls. And according to this teaching, all these powers are exerting an influence upon this world and upon the mind of man. And the whole explanation of the predicament of men individually and collectively, at this moment, is that it is the result of the work and the activity and the efforts of the devil and his powers.

Now we are not given many details about this. All we are told is that the devil was in existence and manifested his power the moment man was created. He was there, indeed, before man. He is an angelic being. All angelic beings were created by God, and he made them all perfect, but we are told of this one who had such great power that in his pride and arrogance he rebelled against God. He was not content to be subservient to God, or to be a servant of God. He wanted to be equal with God. So he rebelled against God, we are told, and persuaded a number of other angels to do the same thing with him, and there you have the devil and the fallen angels. And they are consumed with a passion of antagonism against God. The devil hates God. That was the reason for his fall. But since his fall he has hated God still more. And the devil has really only one ambition, and that is to ruin God's world. God made the world. He made it perfect and as he made man in his own image, man was made perfect. The devil hated it, and he knew that the best way to harm God and his name and his glory, was to ruin God's creation, so he came in and he tempted man, and man in his folly listened to him and he fell. He went into a state of sin and he dragged down the whole cosmos with him.

Now that is the biblical explanation of the trouble. As you see, it started long ago. That is why the Bible starts its history in the Garden of Eden. It is interested primarily in man, in his creation and condition. It says that all the troubles in the world have resulted from that initial mistake and error of man when he listened to the devil, and lifted up himself in pride as the devil had done before him, and down he went dragging the whole creation with him.

So then, according to the Bible, the result is the very thing I have put before you in these various quotations. Man, in listening to the temptation and the enticement of the devil, became the slave of the devil. He became an absolute serf in the devil's hands, and his life ever since has been dominated by the devil. That is why he is called 'the prince of the power of the air', 'the spirit that now worketh in the children of disobedience'. That is why he is called 'the god of this world who blinds'. The whole of the human race has become his slave. He is 'the strong man armed that keepeth his palace', whose 'goods are in peace'.

We must be clear about this. The Bible tells us that the power of the devil is tremendous. That is what makes the world so tragic. It does not even believe in the existence of the devil, and it does not realize, therefore, that all its troubles are due to this tremendous tyrant with his awful power. Listen to the Son of God: 'the strong man armed, keepeth his palace, his goods in peace'. Or take again those words of the apostle Paul in Ephesians 6:12, Do not think, he says, that the problem of living is the problem of flesh and blood. You are not up against merely your own weaknesses or the weaknesses of other men and women; behind all that are the principalities and the powers, the rulers of the darkness of this world, the spiritual wickedness, high in the heavenly places, exerting this awful power upon the entire human race.

There is the explanation, then, but let us take it step by step. I say that it is a tremendous power and I prove it in this way. The power of the devil, the power of evil, is so great that every human being ever born into this world has been defeated by it. Read the Old Testament. There are some very great men there. Abraham and the patriarchs, the prophets and godly people like them, but every one of them sinned. Every one of them fell down before the devil. The Bible puts it as strongly as this. Man, even when he was perfect—Adam, a perfect man, made in the image of God—was defeated by the devil. The devil was so powerful, so subtle. His ingenuity is such that no man has ever been able to stand against him, even a perfect man. The apostle Paul sums it all up by saying, 'There is none righteous, no, not one . . . . For all have sinned, and come short of the glory of God' (Rom 3:10, 23). There has never been a human being in this world that has lived a wholly righteous life and has satisfied God, not one. The whole world, therefore, lieth guilty before God.

Why is this? It is because of the terrible power of the

devil, who dominates and who controls, and who masters. He does so, firstly, through the *mind*. He hates God, and so he persuades the human race to hate him too. I have already quoted 2 Corinthians 4:3 'But if our gospel be hid, it is hid to them that are lost.' The devil does not want anybody to believe in God and in the Son of God, so he blinds their minds. There is nothing new about unbelief. You are not being particularly modern or clever by not being a Christian. There has always been opposition to the gospel. The Bible is full of examples of it. It does not conceal it. No, the gospel has never been believed by men and women en masse in this world. 'Few there be that find it', says our Lord. 'Enter ye in at the strait gate: for wide is the gate, and broad is the way, that leadeth to destruction, and many there be which go in thereat: because strait is the gate, and narrow is the way, which leadeth unto life, and few there be that find it' (Mt 7:13–14). The devil dominates the bulk of the life of mankind. He has always done it, and you know you are not being anything new or different by rejecting this gospel and this preaching and teaching of the Bible. Mankind has always been doing that. The devil has been dominant and he governs the mind.

The Apostle puts it again in that great phrase of his in 1 Corinthians 2:14. He says, 'But the natural man receiveth not the things of the Spirit of God: for they are foolishness unto him: neither can he know them, because they are spiritually discerned.' The clever people of the first century ridiculed the cross as much as the clever people of today do. They did not believe in the Son of God, nor in his atoning death. No, they ridiculed it, and said it was foolishness. It was foolishness to the Greeks, and it is still foolishness to such people. There is nothing new. It is all a manifestation of the devil, dominating the mind of man. He does not allow man to think freely. He keeps him in blinkers. He only lets him see what he wants him to see. And the whole difficulty for man is to see the truth. You try and you soon find and feel something of the power of the devil.

But then he not only controls the mind, he controls the desires. Why is there always sweetness in stolen or prohibited fruit? Why does every child immediately want to do something that his parents tell him not to do? Why is sin so pleasing and so pleasant? Answer that question. Where do these desires come from? The answer given here is that they all come from the devil, and he governs our *actions*, and our *wills*, in exactly the same way. He rebelled against God, and as he wants everybody else to do the same, he persuades everybody else to rebel against God. He makes us hate God, and he makes us hate God's laws. 'The carnal [natural] mind is enmity against God: for it is not subject to the law of God, neither indeed can be' (Rom 8:7). Man by nature is a God-hater. As I have often pointed out, that is the reason why the newspapers are always ready to put it in their pages if they can find a man who has just said that he does not believe in God. In it will go. If they find a Sunday school teacher who has fallen morally, they never fail to say, 'ex-Sunday school teacher has done this or that'. They hate God. They are against him and all his laws. It is because they are dominated by the devil, the hater of God, who is reproducing himself in them.

And he not only dominates the mind and the desire and the will, he dominates the *whole of life*, and he produces a fear. There is a great statement about this made by the author of the epistle to the Hebrews, in the second chapter of his great letter. He puts it like this: 'Forasmuch then as the children are partakers of flesh and blood, he also himself likewise took part of the same; that through death he might destroy him that had the power of death, that is, the devil; and deliver them who through fear of death were all their lifetime subject to bondage' (vv. 14–15). And the long story of the human race shows this fear of death. You find it in your Greek mythology, you find it in all ancient literature, a fear of death. Death is pictured with a scythe coming and ever coming.

Why is mankind afraid of death? What is the cause of this? Well, there is the answer. It is a power exercised by the devil. And he is able to exercise this power because of the law of God. People do not believe in God, or in the law of God. But there is still a relic and a remnant of belief which remains. They have a fear of death because they know that death is followed by judgement and the law condemns us all. Death is the last spectre, which is ever growing nearer. Man would like to evade death if he could, but he cannot. So he is in a kind of bondage. The end is death and he does his best to postpone it. He whistles in the dark. He pretends he does not believe in all this, and yet he does. The fear remains.

Now I can show you all this in a brief picture. Look at the pagan world. Look at it in past centuries, look at it in our own time. It is the picture of a life of fear, fearing the sun and the moon and the stars, fearing their own man-made gods; a life of fear, of squalor, of evil and of sin. That is what the devil is producing. God produces perfection, paradise. The devil produces chaos. He reduces God's order to chaos. That is what the world is today. What God has made is turned by the devil, in his power over the minds of men, and over their hearts and wills, into the chaos with which we are familiar. But, 'God forbid that I should glory, save in the cross of our Lord Jesus Christ . . . .' Why? Because he and he alone, on that cross, has delivered me from that thraldom, that tyranny, that dominion, of Satan and sin.

Now the Son of God came into this world to do that very thing. Let me give it to you in the words of John—I want you to see that these are not my own theories, but that I am just expounding the Scriptures to you—in 1 John 3:8. 'He that committeth sin is of the devil; for the devil sinneth from the beginning. For this purpose the Son of God was manifested, *that he might destroy the works of the devil*' (italics mine). That is why the Son of God came into this world, in order that 'he might destroy the works of the devil'. That is what he himself meant by his words about 'the strong man armed', and of the time when the one stronger than he should come. All humanity was too weak to fight the devil, he had beaten us all, he had clubbed us on the head, and we none of us could get out of that castle, that palace of his. It needed somebody stronger, and now he has come, the Son of God has come that he might destroy the works of the devil. That is why he was manifested.

Have you, I wonder, ever worked that out, and followed as it is depicted in the pages of the four Gospels? When you read your Gospel, do you just see our Lord fighting human beings? Well if that is all you see, you are a very superficial reader of your Bible. Do you not see him fighting this power that is behind men? Do you not see him engaged in this mortal combat with the devil? What an epic it is, what a fight, what a crusade. The Son of God has come—what for? To fight the devil, because the devil is the master of man. The moment Jesus was born, the devil tried to deal with him, did he not? Do you remember the edict that was sent out by a king called Herod, that all male children under two years should be murdered? Why? He was trying to murder this one, the Son of God, who had been born as a baby in Bethlehem. The fight began the moment that our Lord was born. And it continued. Look at him tempted forty days and forty nights in the wilderness. What is this? It is the devil trying to get him down. 'All these things [the kingdoms of the world] will I give thee, if thou will fall down and worship me' [Mt 4:9). He is trying to bring him down, to make him bow the knee to him, he is trying to get him down as he got Adam down. Again, look at the fight as our Lord meets cases of devil-possession and sickness and illness, and all the ravages of sin and evil. There he is, fighting the battle, to release people from sin's foul bondage.

Then, look at our Lord in the Garden of Gethsemane, sweating great drops of blood on to the ground. What is this? He is in agony, he is struggling. What does it mean? Oh, he knows that before he can really deal with this enemy he has got to pass through the terrible moment when he no longer sees the face of God, and the thought makes him sweat blood. It is the conflict against the devil which culminates on the cross, with the devil attacking the whole time.

Our Lord came, then, into this world in order to rid us from the tyranny and from the power of the devil. But it was on the cross that he did it supremely and finally. This is the thing that I want to hold before you. Did you ever notice those words in John 12:31–33? 'Now is the judgment of this world: now shall the prince of this world be cast out. And I, if I be lifted up from the earth, will draw all men unto me. This he said, signifying what death he should die.' What is happening in his death is the judgement of this world—we saw that earlier—and also, in his death he is going to defeat the prince of this world: 'Now shall the prince of this world be cast out.'

This is the great and wonderful story. Have you ever been filled with a sense of amazement and wonder at the drama of the cross? Have you ever looked at it like this? We have been surveying the cross, and we have seen different aspects coming forth. Have you ever looked at it in these terms— the drama, the conflict, the fight? How did our Lord ever come to such a place, what brought him there? Ah, you say, that was men who did not understand him. Is that a sufficient and an adequate answer? My dear friend, can you not see the devil behind men? What was the offence of Jesus of Nazareth? To whom did he do any harm? What was wrong with his teaching? What was wrong with his miracles? What was wrong with his acts of kindness? He came to do good, he came to teach, he came to deliver mankind. What reception did he get? Well, look at it in the Pharisees and scribes, look at their bitterness and hatred, look at their scorn and their derision, look at their blasphemy. Look at it not only there, but also in the Roman governor, Pilate. Look at it in King Herod, the King of the Jews, look at it in the common people. Can you not see this terrible blasphemy, this scorn? Why all this feeling, why all this hatred, why all this vituperation? There is only one explanation. It is the devil that is fighting. It is the devil in these men and women.

But let me come right up to date. Why do you think it is a clever thing not to be a Christian? What is wrong with Christianity? What is wrong with this blessed person? What is wrong with his teaching? What is your objection? Why do you think it is clever to reject? Why do you blaspheme it? Why do you pour scorn upon it? Why do you hate it? There is only one answer. You are the unconscious victim of the devil. It is the hatred of the devil that is coming out in you. You cannot produce reasons for your hatred. This is the most extraordinary thing in this matter. You see it running right through the records in the four Gospels. Read the account of what happened to him: 'And when they had plaited a crown of thorns, they put it upon his head, and a reed in his right hand: and they bowed the knee before him, and mocked him, saying, Hail, King of the Jews! And they spit upon him, and took the reed, and smote him on the head. And after they had mocked him, they took the robe off from him, and put his own raiment on him, and led him away to crucify him' (Mt 27:29–31). Or again, 'And they that passed by'—when he is actually nailed to the tree—'reviled him, wagging their heads and saying, Thou that destroyest the temple, and buildest it in three days, save thyself. If thou be the Son of God, come down from the cross. Likewise also the chief priests mocking him, with the scribes and elders, said, He saved others; himself he cannot save. If he be the King of Israel, let him now come down from the cross, and we will believe him. He trusted in God; let him deliver him now, if he will have him: for he said, I am the Son of God. The thieves also, which were crucified with him, cast the same in his teeth' (vv. 39–44).

Where are you, expert psychologists? How do you explain that? Here is an innocent man. Nobody can bring any evidence against him. He has done no wrong. Indeed, he has done nothing but good in the world. He came to help people and to teach, but look at the spite, look at the mocking and the spitting and the jeering and the scoffing. What is the matter with them? There is only one answer to the question—he gave it himself. He said, 'But this is your hour, and the power of darkness' (Lk 22:53); these people do not know what they are doing. That is why he prayed on the cross and said, 'Father, forgive them; for they know not what they do' (Lk 23:34). And, indeed, they did not know what they were doing.

Would you hate a man like this, a man who has done no harm, and no wrong to anybody at all, a man who was always going about doing good? Would you treat him like this? Would you not make a protest? Would you join the jeering, mocking throng, would you spit upon him? I say it is unnatural. Of course it is! It is hellish, it is the devil, it is evil incarnate. They knew not what they did: 'This is your hour, and the power of darkness', and this is the wonder of it all. The world was very pleased with itself, was it not, as it looked upon him there dying upon the cross? That is why they laugh. That is why they are joking. Can you not see it, can you not see their faces? Have you got enough imagination? 'Come down,' they say, 'you who say you are the Son of God. You who claim to save others, come down, save yourself. He cannot save himself. Wonderful! At last we have got rid of him.'

The chief priests and scribes, of course, were particularly delighted. In their council they had said: 'What do we? for this man doeth many miracles. If we let him thus alone, all men will believe on him: and the Romans shall come and take away both our place and nation.'

But there was a very clever politician among them, a man called Caiaphas. He thought this was very wonderful. He said, 'Ye know nothing at all, nor consider that it is expedient for us, that one man should die for the people, and that the whole nation perish not' (Jn 11: 47–50). Let them kill him, he said, then we will be all right. Let us make a scapegoat of him. We will hide behind him. Once they have got rid of him, all will be well for us. Everybody was pleased, the whole world was delighted. At last they had got him, they had nailed him, they had killed him. He was finished.

Was he? 'Having spoiled principalities and powers, he made a shew of them openly, triumphing over them in it.' And yet, here they are, they think they have reached the hour of victory, they have got this one whom they hate and the devil was delighted. If only he could kill him, that would be the end. And that was his terrible miscalculation. He did not realize, and this is the devil's great blunder, that by bringing the Son of God to the cross he was defeating himself, and bringing about his own ultimate doom. How? Well, the Apostle tells us that our Lord there on the cross, in apparent weakness, was putting the devil and his powers to an open shame and that he was triumphing over them.

And the Lord does it in this way. The power of the devil is, after all, nothing but a usurped power. He has no power of his own. The devil is the god of this world, the prince of the power of the air, for one reason only, and that is that man in sin has gone out of the kingdom of God, and is therefore in the kingdom of the devil. The devil has no power over man, except that man is estranged from God, and is no longer in touch with the power of God. The only one who can master the devil is God. And the moment we are out of touch with God, we are mastered by the devil, and we are his helpless tools, and victims in his kingdom like goods in a palace. And that is the position of the entire human race. The entire human race sinned in Adam and it became the slave of the devil, as I have shown you. And we all continue by nature to be slaves of the devil. We are alienated from God, we are under the wrath of God, and we are outside the kingdom of God, so we are absolutely helpless in the hands of the devil.

'The strong man armed keepeth ... his goods at peace.' When he rules his palace his goods are at peace. There is only one power that can deliver a man out of the clutches of hell and of the devil. It is the power of God. But how can I have that power? I have sinned against God, I am a rebel against him. God's wrath is upon me. Before I can know the power of God I must be reconciled to God. And that was the very thing that was happening on the cross on Calvary's hill. What stands between every one of us and God is the broken law of God. We have broken God's law, we have insulted him, we have spat upon him, and his condemnation is upon us, and we must be delivered from this and reconciled to God before we will ever know the power that can set us free. That is exactly what happened on the cross. That is why those two verses in Colossians go together: 'Blotting out the handwriting of ordinances that was against us, which was contrary to us, and took it out of the way, nailing it to his cross'; and then he 'spoiled principalities and powers'.

The two things belong together.

There on the cross our Lord was reconciling us unto God. 'God was in Christ, reconciling the world to himself, not imputing their trespasses unto them' (2 Cor 5:19). Christ had to pay this penalty; the law had to have its way; and he has borne the punishment. And because of that, if we believe in him we are free from the punishment, and free of the condemnation. We are reconciled to God, and the power of God takes over and delivers us from the devil and his cohorts, and transfers us into the kingdom of God. That is why the Apostle puts it like this in Colossians 1:13, 'Who hath delivered us from the power of darkness, and hath translated us into the kingdom of his dear Son.' That is how it happens. That is what was happening upon the cross. The devil thought he was defeating Christ, but Christ was reconciling us to God, defeating the devil and delivering us out of his clutches. He does it by paying the penalty and putting us right with God. The power of God comes into us and we are born again, receiving new natures, and becoming new people. The Holy Spirit is put within us, and Christ's presence is ever at hand to help us.

That is why John was able to say, 'and the whole world lieth in wickedness', but 'the wicked one toucheth him not'. He not only touches the world, he embraces it, and the world cannot get out of his clutches. But Christ takes us out of his clutches, puts us into his own kingdom, and the devil cannot touch us. He can frighten us perhaps, he can shout at us, but he cannot touch us. That is why the apostle Paul says in Romans 6:14, 'Sin shall not have dominion over you: for ye are not under the law, but under grace.' The one who is stronger than the strong man armed has come, and he has robbed him of his armour wherein he trusted and he has divided his spoil. Oh, what a fool the devil was! How ignorant, how blinded, how puffed up by his own conceit and pride. He thought he was finishing Christ. He was really bringing about his own defeat. Christ has conquered him. 'Now shall the prince of this world be cast out,' and he was.

Let me explain this a little more. Before our Lord died upon the cross, the whole world was in the power of the devil, apart from the Jews, the Children of Israel. One day, some Greeks came along and they said, 'We would see Jesus.' He says, no, not yet, I have got to be 'lifted up' before I can bring in you Gentiles.

The devil controlled the nations of the world, apart from God's own people, until the cross. After the cross, our Lord said, 'If I be lifted up I shall draw all men unto me.' This means men of *all* nations. And he did. From the moment of the cross the Gentiles began to believe and to enter into the kingdom of God. Before, they were outside, and they were in the darkness of heathendom and paganism. Christ died, and he became the Saviour of the world. He draws all men, men of all nations, and of kindreds and of climes unto himself.

So, you see, that what he said himself has literally proved to be the case. From the moment he died upon the cross and ascended into heaven and sent down the Holy Spirit, the gospel was preached everywhere. Men and women like the Galatians—who were not Jews, but pagans and Gentiles, ignorant and benighted, and besotted in sin—were drawn and claimed, and set free from the power of the devil. The same had happened to people in Corinth. Do you remember how the great Apostle reminds them of what they were? 'Be not deceived,' he says, about this, 'neither fornicators, nor idolaters, nor adulterers, nor effeminate, nor abusers of themselves with mankind, nor thieves, nor covetous, nor drunkards, nor revilers, nor extortioners, shall inherit the kingdom of God. And such were some of you: but ye are washed, but ye are sanctified, but ye are justified in the name of the Lord Jesus, and by the Spirit of our God' (1 Cor 6:9–10).

'I am not ashamed of the gospel of Christ: for it is the power of God unto salvation', says Paul to the Romans (1:16), and there is no other power that can save us. That was the power that was released upon the cross, and the testimony of the saints of the centuries has been that Christ has set us free.

> The prisoner leaps to lose his chains;
> The weary find eternal rest,
> And all the sons of want are blest.
>
> *I. Watts*

Here is one of the most wonderful things about the cross. Here is one of the most glorious reasons for glorying in the cross. Here Christ defeated our ultimate enemy, the devil, the one who originally brought man and the universe down. He was cast out, he was defeated. He has been put in chains. And finally, he is going to be completely and utterly destroyed. He will be cast into the lake of fire with the beasts and all the false prophets. And he will have no more power. And:

> Jesus shall reign where'er the sun
> Does his successive journeys run;
> His kingdom stretch from shore to shore,
> Till moons shall wax and wane no more.
>
> *I. Watts*

Have you seen 'the conqueror renowned' as you have looked at the cross? Have you seen him now? If you have, you will join me in saying these words:

> Onward march, all-conquering Jesus.
>   Gird thee on thy mighty sword.
> Sinful earth can ne'er oppose thee,

Hell itself quails at thy word.
Thy great name is so exalted,
Every foe shrinks back in fear.
Terror creeps through all creation,
When it knows that thou art near.

William Williams

Do you see him there at the cross, taking these principalities and powers and the devil, and putting them to an open shame; triumphing over them in it; ridiculing them, and defeating them; smashing them? At the moment when they were glorifying in their own victory, they were finally and completely defeated and routed.

O Jesus, King most wonderful,
Thou Conqueror renowned,
Thou Sweetness most ineffable,
In whom all joys are found!

Bernard of Clairvaux

'God forbid that I should glory, save in the cross of our Lord Jesus Christ.'

Chapter 6

'He Is Our Peace'

In the Cross of Christ I glory,
Towering o'er the wrecks of time.

J. Bowring

Thank God that the Christian can sing words like that in a world like this. Let us now try to find some further reasons why we can do so, and why it is possible for all to do so, if they but believe the gospel of our Lord and Saviour Jesus Christ. So let us return to Galatians 6:14: 'But God forbid that I should glory, save in the cross of our Lord Jesus Christ, by whom the world is crucified unto me and I unto the world.' There is no hope for this world apart from the gospel and the essence of the gospel, as we have seen, is this message about the cross.

Now the author of the hymn which we have just quoted tells us all that he found in the cross. Whatever his mood, or state or condition, the cross sanctified it all: pain or pleasure, whatever was happening to him. The cross always speaks. That is the Apostle's position. He glories in this because he has discovered that whatever is happening to him, this is the message that is always with him, and that turns everything to his advantage, and so he makes his boast in the cross.

Now we have been examining the various things that the

Apostle here, and in other places in his writings, tells us about the cross. But still we have not finished. 'God forbid that I should glory,' says the Apostle, 'save in the cross.' There is no end to it. It is such a tremendous thing, and so I move forward now to give one further reason which the Apostle has for glorying in the cross of the Lord Jesus Christ. This is that it is the cross of our Lord Jesus Christ that alone can produce true unity and a real peace among men. Now it is to that I want to call your attention, and what a time it is to consider this, because everybody's mind is engaged on the whole question of how to produce unity in the world. The assassination of the late President Kennedy* pinpoints that in a very acute manner for us.

Now I am not going to preach on President Kennedy, but it would be madness not to see what that terrible event, that awful event, should make us all think about. He was a man who was struggling and striving in various ways to bring men and women together. There are those who would say that he met his death because he was trying to solve the problem of integration in the United States. Black and white and coloured—how to bring them together. How to bring an end to segregation, and how to produce integration. It was certainly one of the problems with which he was struggling. He went to Texas because he was concerned about that. Then he faced the problem of the two groupings of the nations of the world, the Iron Curtain between them. He was striving, he was struggling with this problem of how to bring together these two warring factions of human nature and of humankind. Here was a man who gave his life and his activity to that very question, to that very matter. And I have no doubt that it is true to say that in many ways he met his death because of these things. We are concerned, then, with

*This sermon was preached in 1963 shortly after the assassination of President Kennedy.

this problem. We are in a world which is full of tension, full of divisions, full of strife, full of the danger of war. We are in a world that is divided up hopelessly, a world of unhappiness and pain.

The Bible has always said that this world is an evil world. Nothing else says that, the newspapers do not say it, the newspapers regard an event such as President Kennedy's assassination, as exceptional. It is only exceptional in the one sense that it happens to be unusually dramatic. But the world is full of that kind of thing. That is the sort of world we are living in. The world seems shocked because of the unexpected. It is not unexpected. It is not unusual. This is 'this present evil world' as the Bible calls it. I am not exaggerating this particular thing. I have my own views with regard to whoever may have committed this dastardly crime, but I do maintain that this is but one of the manifestations of a strife, a warfare, an antagonism, a bitterness and a hatred. It is just a particularly ugly manifestation of it. But the thing itself belongs to a whole category which is, alas, the cause of our greatest troubles in this world today. And that is why I am calling attention to it.

Now I want to look at it, not only in terms of the world situation, but also in terms of our individual lives. One of the greatest fallacies today is that we draw too sharp a distinction between the individual and the mass, between nations and persons or individuals. A nation is nothing after all but a collection of individuals, or you might say that it is nothing but the individual writ large. The world is a sort of macrocosm of which man is a microcosm, and what is true of the nations of the world is true of individuals. There are groupings and divisions within all the nations, and divisions and groupings and antagonisms and tensions in yet smaller units, even in families—divisions, strife, disagreement, misunderstanding. But we can take it even further. How many of you know perfect rest? How many know real peace and quiet? Is there not a warfare going on in you? Is there not a strife and a tension, is there not a conflict? We have to say there is— we are all born like that. We are born creatures of conflict, within and without, in every realm and department of life. And what I want to try to demonstrate is that there is only one thing in the whole world at this moment that can deal with this warfare and tension and strife. It is the cross of our Lord and Saviour, Jesus Christ.

If you read the second chapter of Paul's epistle to the Ephesians, you will notice what the Apostle had to say there. It was not surprising that he gloried in the cross, because the cross of the Lord Jesus Christ had done what he regarded as the most wonderful and amazing thing that he had ever known—it had produced the Christian church. Why is this so wonderful? It is wonderful for the reason that together, side by side in the Christian church, there were Jews and Gentiles. Now that was the thing that never failed to amaze the Apostle. You remember that the ancient world was divided up into Jews and all the rest, the Gentiles. The Jews despised the Gentiles, and would refer to them as dogs. The Gentiles, too, had their own view of the Jews, and it appeared to be an utter impossibility that they could ever come together. There was, as the Apostle says in that very chapter, a middle wall of partition between them.

The wall in Berlin, you see, is not the first wall that has been built in this world to separate people from one another. The world has always had its iron curtains. We change the terminology but the fact has always been there: the middle wall of partition, Jews one side, Gentiles the other side, and, between them, a bitter hatred and animosity, which we can scarcely even imagine. The apostle Paul, before his conversion, was one of the most bitter Jews the world has ever known. He was a Jew who revelled in it and prided himself in it, and he despised the Gentiles. But the extraordinary thing he finds is that in the Christian church Jews and Gentiles are found together and the middle wall of partition, as he says, has been broken down. He keeps on repeating that in the epistle to the Ephesians. He says in Ephesians 1:11, 13: 'In whom also we have obtained an inheritance, being predestinated according to the purpose of him who worketh all things after the counsel of his own will .... In whom ye also trusted'—*we*, being the Jews, *you also*, the Gentiles—'after that ye heard the word of truth ....'

And then, as we saw in the second chapter, let me remind you, he said in effect, 'Wherefore, remember, that ye being in time past Gentiles in the flesh, who are called Uncircumcision by that which is called the Circumcision in the flesh made by hands; that at that time ye were without Christ, being aliens from the commonwealth of Israel, and strangers from the covenants of promise, having no hope, and without God in the world: But now in Christ Jesus ye who sometimes [at one time] were far off are made nigh by the blood of Christ. For he is our peace, who hath made both one, and hath broken down the middle wall of partition between us; having abolished in his flesh the enmity, even the law of commandments contained in ordinances; for to make in himself of twain one new man, so making peace' (2:11–15).

Now this to the Apostle was the most amazing and astounding thing conceivable. The impossible had happened: Jew and Gentile had been brought together, and there was one new man in the Christian church worshipping the same God and glorying in the same Saviour.

That is therefore one of the chief reasons why he gloried in the cross of Christ. And it is that which I want to expound to you. Let me do it like this. What is the cause of the divisions and the enmities that characterize the life of this world? Is that not the big question that comes up at this time? I am not going to talk politics to you or even pay tribute to the late President Kennedy, that is not what I am called upon to do. Others do that kind of thing. The Christian preacher must deal with causes and, thank God, in the light of this book we can do so in a manner which is something that the statesman cannot do, because (and I say this to the glory of God) here is the only explanation.

What is the cause of the division? What is the cause of the unhappiness that is in the world today? Why is the world as it is? Why have we had these wars? Why are the nations preparing for a further war? Why is there tragedy and trouble and discord? And there is only one answer to all the questions. It is the pride of the natural, unregenerate human heart. Pride, nothing else. Let me show you how it works. The Bible is full of this teaching. Away back at the very beginning it gives us the story of how one brother murdered another brother. Cain murdered Abel. Why did he do it? He did it because of jealousy, and jealousy is the child of pride. There it is right away back at the very beginning, and it has gone on ever since. This old book is full of accounts of that kind of thing. There are foolish people today who say that you should not give the Old Testament to a child to read because of the terrible things you find there, the sins of David and stories like that. That is just the point. The Bible is an honest book, a realistic one which tells you the truth. It shows human nature as it is and it conceals nothing. Pride shows itself in all kinds of ways. Take the prophet Jeremiah. He has a great statement about all this. He was given clear insight by God to see the cause of trouble, and he puts it like this. 'Thus saith the Lord, Let not the wise man glory in his wisdom, neither let the mighty man glory in his might, let not the rich man glory in his riches':—glory means boast, remember—'But let him that glorieth glory in this, that he understandeth and knoweth me, that I am the Lord which exercise lovingkindness, judgment, and righteousness, in the earth: for in these things I delight, saith the Lord' (Jer 9:23–24).

Then you come over to the New Testament, and you get exactly the same thing. The apostle Paul, in writing to the Corinthians, shows how the world in his time was divided up not only into Jew and Gentile, but it was divided up into Greeks and barbarians, wise and unwise, too. The world has always been like this. You will find it again in Ephesians 2, and then you have an extraordinary statement of the same thing by the Apostle in Philippians 3. Read this little bit of autobiography that he gives us. He says, 'For we are the circumcision, which worship God in the spirit, and rejoice in Christ Jesus, and have no confidence in the flesh. Though,' he says, 'I might also have confidence in the flesh. If any other man thinketh that he hath whereof he might trust in the flesh, I more: Circumcised the eighth day, of the stock of Israel, of the tribe of Benjamin, an Hebrew of the Hebrews; as touching the law, a Pharisee; concerning zeal, persecuting the church; touching the righteousness which is in the law, blameless' (3:4–6). There he was, proud of it all.

Now these are but some of the texts which we have in the Scriptures, and there are many more, which show us that the essential cause of all the strife and the unhappiness and the tension in the world, and ultimately, all the tragedy, both in individuals and in the life of nations and groups within the nations, all these are the result of pride. How does it work? Well let me take you through the sorry catalogue, and if we do not use a time such as this to do that, then I say we have failed, and failed completely. What do men and women take pride in and what is it that causes this pride of theirs to lead to divisions?

Well, as we are told, they take pride in their *birth*, and in their race. You remember how Kipling spoke about 'the lesser breeds without the law'. Pride of birth, pride of race, pride of nationality, pride of colour—black and white. This is the tension in the world today, this is a part of the trouble. It may not be the only cause of the tragedy that has taken place, but men are standing apart because of these things. Human beings, souls in the sight of God, but divided by colour, black and white; and remember, there are these elements on both sides. But you get this trouble with respect to nationality, with respect to race, with respect to the accident of birth, and all these things. All those matters that the Apostle enumerates there, in Ephesians 2 and in Philippians 3. Now the Apostle himself, before he became an Apostle and before he became a Christian, delighted in these things. He was proud of them, and of the fact that he was an Hebrew of the Hebrews. He looked down upon everybody who was not. He was born into a particular tribe, the tribe of Benjamin, and he was filled with pride in all this.

Another cause of strife is *power* pride in one's power. How much tension is there in the world today between the 'haves' and the 'have nots'? Those who have want to hold on to what they have got. Those who have not, want it. And each one is consumed with an equal passion, and inevitably you get strife and tension, with people wanting something, and wanting to hold on to something. Now this is true of nations. It has been one of the most prolific causes of wars, particularly in the present century, but it has been a cause of wars long before that. Greed, the desire to have, to have power, to be great, to be wonderful. Wealth, and the power of wealth. It is the cause of so much industrial strife. Employer and employed—the employed want a greater share of that which has hitherto been the possession of the employers, and each side becomes rigid. So you get tension and strife, you get division, and ultimately you get war. But it is all the result of pride. Power is a wonderful thing.

Nations get drunk on power. Individuals get drunk on it too, and once they have it, they want to hold it. 'Uneasy lies the head that wears the crown.' Lust for power, and for domination. The whole of human history is redolent of this kind of thing, and pride of power does it.

And then pride of *intellect* does exactly the same thing. We have seen how the ancient world was divided up into Greeks and barbarians, the wise and the unwise. The Greeks were a very intellectual people, as well as a people of great military prowess. They had produced that succession of mighty philosophers, the greatest philosophers the world has ever known, and they were proud of it. So they looked round at all the other nations of the world, and they said What do they know? What do they understand? What philosophy have they got? Some of them are good at fighting, some of them are good at business, some of them are good at navigation, but they do not understand. So they divided up the whole world into Greeks and barbarians, and the wise and the unwise.

But again, here was rivalry and tension, stress and strain, and it is as common in the world today as it was then. These subtle divisions and distinctions permeate through the whole of life. I have come across many cases in this world where this very thing has caused grave agony, even within families. It happens that one member of the family, being a bit brighter than the rest, goes on with his education. He goes to a university, and the others do not. I have known that lead to heartache, and almost heartbreak, in certain families. Intellect, the pride of the man who has got it and is given an opportunity, and the others, feeling a certain amount of jealousy and envy. 'Who is he?' they say, 'Because he has got a little knowledge, does he think he is different?' And so on. You must be aware of all this, it is one of the many social problems that are worrying the minds of the authorities in this country at the present time.

Those, then, are the three main ways in which this pride that is in man, because he is a sinner, has manifested itself throughout the running centuries. The next step in the argument is that there is nothing known to the world today that can deal with that situation. Now that is a very strong statement to make, is it not? But I make it. The state of the world at this moment is an absolute proof of that, in and of itself. The world can never make peace. All the world can do is to put an end, or at least put a stop for the time being, to actual war. The world at its best has never produced anything beyond a temporary cessation of hostilities. It can produce nothing but a kind of armed interval, in which we are not actually fighting.

But you see the whole fallacy behind what the world is doing is that it does not realize that merely not to fight is not peace. Peace is positive, not negative. Peace means love, sympathy, understanding, a true unity, and the world knows nothing about it, and it cannot produce it. Now this is to me a most vital and important thing for it shows how it is that the world must inevitably fail. But the world fools itself, because it regards the cessation of hostilities as positive peace. Let me give you an illustration of this. In the first world war they used poison gas in fighting one another. But did you realize that in the second world war, they did not use it? Some of us remember receiving instructions in 1938 about what to do if mustard gas, etc, were used, but it was never used. Why not? Was it because the world has advanced? Was it because man at last has got love in his heart towards his fellow man? No. There was only one answer. Both sides had mustard gas, and each side knew that if they used it, the other would retaliate. Therefore, neither side used it. That was not peace, that was just the avoidance of doing something that was going to do you harm. There is no advance, there is no development, and I think there is a real case for saying that what has given us what we call peace since the end of the last war in 1945, is not that the nations of the world are any more intelligent than they were, or any more loving than they were, or that they have come any nearer to one another than they were. There is only one thing that has done it, and that is the possession of the atom bombs on the two sides. Was that not what solved the Cuban missile crisis? The two sides knew that if one used it the other would retaliate and they would both suffer, so they did not use it.

But that is not peace, that is fear. That is not what we really mean by peace. Peace, I say, is something positive. Peace means a new attitude, a new understanding. Peace means a love. But the world, even at its best, is incapable of producing it. Or take another argument. There are certain people in this country who say 'better be red than dead'. Let this country go in for unilateral disarmament, anything is better than war, they say. And they are prepared to do that. But you see that again is no solution, because if you did that, what would happen is that one section of the world would be dominated by another. That is not peace. When a bullet keeps everybody else down, there is no fighting, but it is not peace. The weakling is just dominated by the bully, and if you go in for unilateral disarmament that is the inevitable result. You will be governed by the reds, or, if the red gives in, he will be governed by the rest. That is not peace, that is domination. That is the peace that comes from the death of everything that is most glorious in human nature, that is serfdom. You do not get wars in places where there is serfdom, you do not even get strikes. But that is not peace, because it is entirely negative.

Not only that, take all the efforts that are being made in the world, and as you look at them and as you examine

141

them, you see behind them a spirit of hatred, and enmity, a spirit of strife. Let us be realistic and face the facts. The late President Kennedy was hated and reviled by many of his own fellow countrymen—not only by the man who performed this murderous act, but by many others, by good and respectable people who hated him because of his very policies—and there is animosity and hatred on both sides.

So when you look at the world, even at its best and at its highest, you see at once that it does not produce any peace. I have to say, in order to be honest and to be plain, that some of the most bitter men I have ever met in my life, have been pacifists. I have never seen such bitter hatred in the hearts of men as in some pacifists I have known. They have been impossible to get on with, impossible to work with. They have been animated by a spirit of hatred against militarism. But that is not peace. While there is bitterness in your heart you have not got peace. No, the world cannot produce peace. The world can never bring down the middle walls of partition. It can produce a kind of gentlemanly appearance of peace, it can succeed in having a cessation of hostilities, only because it is wise and politic and utilitarian to do so. But it is always waiting for the opportunity, and one only has to produce some invention before anyone else for the antagonism to appear. Can you believe the words of nations, can you believe the solemn pledges and vows? The history of the world gives the lie direct to any such assumption.

Oh no, if this century has done nothing else, it has done this. It has proved, absolutely and beyond any controversy, that man cannot be taught by education to live in a peaceable manner, and to love his friends and his enemies. Now there was a great argument that that could be done. The late Mr H. G. Wells was the outstanding proponent of this theory. War, he and others taught, can be banished, if only you educate people. It is ignorant people who fight, they said, and the more ignorant they are, the more they fight. It is ignorance that causes people to fight. Educate them, show them the folly of war, show them the monstrosity, and the evil of it, show them that nothing ever comes of war but harm and suffering, maiming and bitterness, and all the rest. Show them that, and they will burn all their arms, and they will all embrace one another, and there will never be another war. Poor man! The last war convinced him, so he wrote his last book, and called it *Mind at the End of its Tether*. It was the end of the tether and beyond it. This, the most educated of all the centuries, has been the most bloody, and never has the world been so full of war and tension and strife and dispute as it is at this very time. Man cannot produce peace. Man cannot bring the opposites together, because, as I have been trying to show you, the trouble is in the heart of man, not in his mind, but in his heart. It is his passion, it is lust, it is desire, it is pride. Man's pride is greater than his understanding, and in order to please his own pride and to pamper it, he will do things that in his inner man he knows to be wrong. Pride is the biggest power in the world, and nothing that is known to man can deal with the problem of pride. That is why I assert again that there is only one thing in the world at this moment that can give peace and unity, that can bring men and women together and give us any hope of real true peace, and that is the cross of Christ. That is why the Apostle gloried in it.

How does the cross do this? It is really perfectly simple, and the gospel *is* simple because it always gets to the root of the problem, and, having got to the root of the problem, it does not waste its time in trying various expedients. It knows there is only one way of peace and it comes straight to it. The first thing the cross does is to show us to ourselves. Of course, we always defend ourselves, do we not? It isn't my fault, we say, it is his. If only he understood. Or take husbands and wives, when they separate from one another. You listen to the story of the husband: 'This woman is impossible!' Then you listen to the woman: 'That man of mine, I could not live with him, he is an impossible man!' It is always somebody else, is it not? We are never wrong, we are very wonderful, if only we could be understood. The trouble is people do not understand us. We are all people of peace. None of us wants to quarrel with anybody, we are not jealous, or envious, we are not quarrelsome. It is always somebody else, always that other person. Do you know what the gospel does? What the cross does? It shows you to yourself. And nothing else in the whole world does that but the cross. There is nothing that will ever humble a man or a nation but the cross of Christ. I have tried to show you that everything else inevitably fails. But the cross tells us the simple plain truth about ourselves.

Think of it like this. Why did the Son of God ever come into this world? Why did he leave the courts of glory? Why was he born as a little babe? Why did he take unto him human nature? There is only one answer. He came because man could not save himself. He said that. 'The Son of man,' he says, 'is come to seek and to save that which was lost' (Lk 19:10). And when I look at that cross and see him dying there, what he tells me is this: you have nothing whereof to boast. The cross tells me that I am a complete failure, and that I am such a failure that he had to come from heaven, not merely to teach and preach in this world, but to die on that cross. Nothing else could save us. I could not keep his teaching. How could I obey the teaching of the Lord Jesus Christ in the Sermon on the Mount, I who cannot live up to my own code, who cannot please other people? It is impossible. We cannot keep ordinary rules, we cannot keep the law of England, leave alone imitate Christ in his perfection. He condemns us completely and absolutely.

Look at this man, the apostle Paul, look at him as Saul of Tarsus. There he was, proud and boastful, yes, 'circumcised the eighth day, of the stock of Israel, of the tribe of Benjamin, an Hebrew of the Hebrews; as touching the law, a Pharisee; concerning zeal, persecuting the church; touching the right-eousness which is in the law, blameless', the perfect man, absolutely moral, absolutely religious, a most learned man, chief of the Pharisees. And then he met this Christ. One glimpse of that blessed face humbled him to the dust, and the light that Christ by the Spirit cast upon the very law which he thought he knew so well, convinced him immedi-ately that he had not kept it. He had missed one little word in the law, the word 'covet'. 'Thou shalt not covet'—he had never seen it.

Here was the great expert on the law, who had studied it all his life, was top in the examinations always, in every test which was given in knowledge of the law, and he had never seen it. He says, 'I had not known sin, but by the law: for I had not known lust, except the law had said, Thou shalt not covet' (Rom 7:7). But the moment he saw that he was finished. 'For I was alive without the law once:'—I thought I was perfect. I thought I was satisfactory before God—'but when the commandment came, sin revived, and I died' (v.9). And the man who had thought he was perfect is heard cry-ing out, 'Oh wretched man that I am! who shall deliver me from the body of this death?' (v.29). He is in a muddle, in utter confusion. 'The good that I would I do not: but the evil which I would not, that I do. Now if I do that I would not, it is no more I that do it, but sin that dwelleth in me. I find then a law, that, when I would do good, evil is present with me. For I delight in the law of God after the inward man; but I see another law in my members, warring against the law of my mind, and bringing me into captivity to the law of sin

145

which is in my members. Oh, wretched man that I am! who shall deliver me from the body of this death?' (vv.19–24). That is what the cross of Christ showed him. It showed him that he was a complete, utter, absolute failure, in word, thought and deed. He had nothing to be proud of. He was a wretched abominable failure. The cross had humbled him and crushed him to the ground. Once you see yourself like that, you forget other people.

But there is more. The cross also reveals to us the truth about others. It makes of twain one new man, it deals with both of us, which is why it is so wonderful. I myself have got to be put down first. It is no use until I am humbled, until I stop saying, 'I am all right, it is the other man.' I am put down, but then it helps me to see the other man also. The cross shows me that these other people also are souls, that it does not matter what the colour of their skin is, or whether they are wealthy or poor, whether they are very learned or very ignorant. It does not matter whether they are very powerful or very weak, they are souls. They are men and women, like me, made originally in the image of God, and standing before God in all the dignity of human nature. But why do they behave as they do? That is the question, and, before I myself was humbled, I never went beyond that. I said, 'It is because they are wrong. I am right and they are wrong.' I have now seen that I am wrong, altogether wrong, but what of them? Ah, now I am enabled to see them in a new way. They are the victims of the devil even as I was. It is that the devil is controlling them, and as I see this I begin to pity them. In other words, what the cross does is to make us both see ourselves exactly as we are and the moment that happens we see that there is no difference at all between us and other people.

You remember how we used to hear, during the last war, of the wonderful things that were happening here in London, how the Duchess and the Mrs Mops were talking together in a very friendly manner, in the same air raid shelter? That is quite right, for when you are within half a centimetre of death, it does not matter very much who you are, does it? Nor what you are by birth. You may both be dead the next moment. So differences were forgotten. Now the cross does that, it shows us that we are all exactly the same. We are one in sin. We are one in failure. We are one in misery. We are one in helplessness and hopelessness. What is the point of boasting that you are a Jew when you are as much a failure as the Gentile? What is the point of boasting that you have got the law, if you cannot keep it? What is the point of boasting about your great brain, if you do not know how to live? What is the point of boasting about your money and your wealth, if you are miserable in your own heart and soul, and filled with jealousy and envy and malice and spite? What is the use of anything? What is the value of anything? What is the point of everything? The cross humbles us.

> My richest gain I count but loss,
> And pour contempt on all my pride.

It is the cross of Christ that brings us all down to the same place. All have sinned and come short of the glory of God. The differences between nations, and groups within them, and individuals, are nothing, when you look at the cross of Christ. We are all miserable, helpless, hopeless sinners. There is nothing in which we can boast, as the Apostle puts it in Philippians 3:7–9, 'But what things were gain to me, those I counted loss for Christ. Yea doubtless, and I count all things but loss for the excellency of the knowledge of Christ Jesus my Lord: for whom,' he says, 'I have suffered the loss of all things, and do count them but dung, that I may win Christ, and be found in him, not having mine own righteousness, which is of the law, but that which is through the faith of Christ, the righteousness which is of God by faith.'

Once you really see this message of the cross, you see yourself grovelling on the dust and the floor, a miserable failure, a hopeless sinner. You can do nothing, neither can your neighbour, you are together in your complete helplessness and hopelessness. But thank God it does not leave you there. You both look up together into the face of the one and only Saviour, the Saviour of the world, the Lamb of God that taketh away the sin of the world. He is not only the Saviour of the western world, he is also the Saviour of the people the other side of the Iron Curtain, which is why I never preach against Communism, or against anything else. I am not called to preach *against*, I am called to hold a Saviour forth. He can save Communists as well as he can save capitalists. He can save black as well as white. He has come to save souls, the Saviour of the world, 'the Lamb of God which taketh away the sin of the world'. 'For there is none other name under heaven given among men, whereby we must be saved' (Acts 4:12). Here is the only one who can encompass the whole world, the whole universe, and all in utter helplessness can look to him. And this is what is so wonderful about it—it is he who saves. It is not we, but he who saves. It is not even our believing in him that saves us, it is he who saves us. It is his going to that cross, and submitting himself as the Lamb of God, and having our sins put upon him by his Father, and bearing the stroke, the punishment, for us, that is what saves us. He does it all.

There is nothing for anybody to boast in. 'For by grace are ye saved through faith; and that not of yourselves: it is the gift of God: not of works, lest any man should boast' (Eph 2:8–9). We are all paupers, and as 'he is our peace' we are given exactly the same gift. Nobody has got anything to boast about. We have done nothing, we could do nothing. He has done it all. So that Paul in writing to the Romans asks,

'Where is the boasting then? It is excluded' (Rom 3:27). 'He that glorieth, let him glory in the Lord' (1 Cor 1:31). 'What hast thou,' says the scripture, 'that thou didst not receive?' (1 Cor 4:7). You see the cross makes us one in every respect. We are one in sin, we are one in failure, we are one in helplessness, and in hopelessness. We believe in the one and only Saviour together. We receive the same forgiveness, we are equally the children of God. By grace, we share the same divine life, we have the same hope of glory, and we all look with admiration and praise and rejoicing and glory into the face of the same Saviour.

That is the only way that you will ever get peace in this world. That is how 'the middle wall of partition' was broken down between the Jew and the Gentile. What is the point of being a Jew if you cannot keep the law about which you talk so much? None at all. There is no difference. 'All have sinned, and come short of the glory of God.' Here is the hope in this world today and there is none other. While men and nations stand up in their arrogance and self-confidence there will be nothing but spite and malice and hatred and war and bitterness and horror. But the moment any man, any woman, sees the truth as it is in Jesus Christ and him crucified, all that is banished, it becomes dung and loss.

> My richest gain I count but loss,
> And pour contempt on all my pride.

What fools we all are. What have you to boast in? Who are you? How do you live? You tell me you are a great intellectual, and I ask you, how do you live? What if everybody knew the things you do? What if everybody knew the things you think, or the things you play with in your imagination? Where do you stand? You, who are self-satisfied, are you ready to come up and to be cross-examined, and to be honest and admit how you live, and all the jealous, envious, rapacious thoughts, and how you commit murder in your mind? You have not done what that wretched assassin did in Dallas, Texas, the other day, but you have done it in your spirit. You have murdered people. You hate them with a bitter hatred, and that is the thing that is damnable, and which causes the division, and builds the middle walls of partition. But it is only the cross that tells us that. There is nothing that will humble the pride of men, and of nations, except to see the truth as it is revealed by the cross of our Lord Jesus Christ.

But once you have seen it, it will grind you to the dust. You will have nothing to pride yourself in, nothing to boast of, but you will lose your jealousy and your envy. You are one with all sinners, but thank God the cross will show you the way out, and it will lift you up. And lift the others with you. It will make peace, and it will make of twain one new man, so making peace. Together you will be able to go to God with your petitions and with your praise and with your thanksgiving. All the divisions will have gone and you will be one with all who believe the same message, rejoicing in him, and enjoying this new life that he has purchased for you at the cost and the price of his own precious blood.

I wish in many ways that I could believe that the assassination of John F. Kennedy is going to bring the nations of the world together. I know it will not. It cannot. It will probably produce more strife and bitter hatred. But there is a death, there is a murder that once took place, that can reconcile because it reconciles men to God. It reconciles them to one another. Stop thinking in terms of nations, think of yourself first. Is that old pride there, is this the thing that governs you? I pray that God may show us to ourselves in the light of the cross of Christ, that all our ugly pride may go, and that we may see our utter hopelessness and helplessness. I pray that we may look up unto him who loved us so dearly, that he even gave his life voluntarily in order that we might be rescued and saved, reconciled to God, and reconciled to our fellow men and women. God forbid that I should glory in anything save in the death on the cross of our Lord Jesus Christ.

Chapter 7

The Cross of Christ Speaks

So far, in a sense, we have been looking at the cross, 'survey-ing it' with Isaac Watts. An illustration of what we have been doing is what we sometimes do with a great mountain. We can walk round it and see it from different angles, and at times we may wonder whether it is the same mountain. But it is—it depends on the spot from which we are looking at it. We get this view and then that one, and then we find another and yet another .... The bigger the mountain, the greater the number of aspects and the angles from which we can view it and see its majesty, its bigness, its glory.

We have been walking round the cross and looking at the different things which can be seen as we gaze upon it, and survey it and consider it, and look at it. It is right and essen-tial to do so, and we could even have gone on doing that, but I am now turning to a different way. Because according to the Scriptures the cross is a very wonderful thing in this sense—that it is something that speaks to us. Had you ever thought of it like that? There is a passage in Hebrews 12 which talks about this. Where have we come to? asks the author. We are not back at Mount Sinai. No, we are under the new covenant, the new dispensation. Then he gives us this wonderful list of the things to which we have come.

'But ye are come unto Mount Sion, and unto the city of the living God, the heavenly Jerusalem, and to an innumerable company of angels, to the general assembly and church of the firstborn, which are written in heaven, and to God the Judge of all, and to the spirits of just men made perfect, and to Jesus the mediator of the new covenant, and'—mark this —'to the blood of sprinkling, that speaketh better things than that of Abel.' The blood of the cross speaks. It makes a statement.

And you will see in Romans 3:24–26 that you have got this comparable idea. He says: 'Being justified freely by his grace through the redemption that is in Christ Jesus: whom God hath set forth, to be a propitiation through faith in his blood, to declare his righteousness for the remission of sins that are past, through the forbearance of God; to declare, I say . . . .' There is a speaking, there is a declaration, there is a setting forth, there is a proclaiming announcement. Now this is a most wonderful way of looking at the cross of our blessed Lord and Saviour, and it is from that angle and stand point that I want to consider it with you now.

Has the cross of Christ ever spoken to you? Have you heard its message? The cross of Christ preaches. The cross of Christ speaks. The blood of the cross speaks. It has something to say. Have you heard it? This man writing the epistle to the Hebrews rejoices with the apostle Paul. He thanks God that this blood speaks something better than the blood of Abel spoke. You remember the story of Cain and Abel, the first two sons of Adam and Eve and the story of how Cain slew his brother Abel, and shed his blood? He murdered him. And the blood of Abel, spilt there upon the ground, spoke as it cried out for vengeance, cried out for punishment, and for retribution. The blood of Abel spoke. And God tells us through the writer to the Hebrews that is not the blood that you and I have come to. We have come to a blood of sprinkling that 'speaketh better things than that of Abel'. This is why all these men in the New Testament rejoice in it. This is why the saints of the ages have rejoiced in it. The blood speaks, and it speaks the best things that the world has ever heard.

Let me call your attention to some of the things that the cross of Christ, the blood of the cross, speaks and says to men and women today. In other words, let us listen to the cross speaking in the form of exposition. There is nothing that so expounds the truth of God to us as the cross of Christ. The Bible expounds the same truth. The cross of Christ lays it open before us and makes it speak to us. Have you ever listened to the message of the cross? Have you ever regarded it as a sermon, and sat and listened to it, and have you heard what it has to say to you? What an exposition of truth there is in that cross on Calvary's hill!

Now obviously, in looking at it like this from different angles, there are certain things which have to be said over and over again, of necessity, and yet this is the marvel and the wonder of the cross, that how ever many times a man may preach about it, he has never finished preaching about it. There is always something fresh to say, always something new. There is a great central message that is always there, but nothing is so wonderful as to see that one thing in different ways, as I say, from different angles and from different perspectives. And that is why a man like the Apostle sees the glory in it. He says there is no end to this. A man may think at times that he knows all about it, but you will find that he does not.

I hope you will forgive a personal reference here. During these twenty-six years in my Westminster pulpit there have been times when in my utter folly I have wondered, or the devil has suggested to me, that there is nothing more for me to say, that I have preached it all. I thank God that I can now say that I feel I am only at the beginning of it. There is no end to this glorious message of the cross, for there is always something new and fresh and entrancing and moving and uplifting that one has never seen before. We must listen to what it has got to say, and the first thing I hear is that *to be a man is a very important and a very serious thing*. Why is the Son of God there upon that cross? We have established the fact that it is the Son of God who dies. Obviously the whole meaning of the cross lies in that fact and the moment you realize that, you ask this question. Why did the Son of God die? What is he doing there? And the first answer I get as I listen to the cross expounding the truth is that the soul of man is something which is very precious.

You remember our Lord's own teaching about this? He said: 'For what shall it profit a man, if he shall gain the whole world, and lose his own soul? Or what shall a man give in exchange for his soul?' (Mk 8:36–37). The cross talks about the soul of man; our Lord is on the cross because of the preciousness of a man's immortal soul. So at once you see that the cross tells me something about myself, and the nature of this manhood that God has given me. It tells me also about the whole purpose of life in this world. This is my soul, this is the thing that matters. Now my body is important and I must not despise it. Many other things are important, too, in this world. It is no part of the preaching of the gospel to depreciate legitimate things, or to ridicule them. But I would say that it is the business of the gospel to say that it is the soul of man that matters, that part of us that goes on even when we die—something imperishable, something which goes on into eternity. The cross puts tremendous emphasis upon that. He came there, not in order that our bodies might be healed, not in order that we might be better fed or clothed or have more information and knowledge, no, he came to save the soul. 'The Son of man is come to seek and to save that which was lost', and what is lost is man's soul.

Here is this tremendous statement, therefore, coming from the cross to us. Have you heard it, have you realized, that the most important thing about you is this soul of yours? Because, whatever else you may possess in this world, whatever the world may give you, a day is coming when every single one of us is going to be bereft of all that, even of the body. We will have to leave it behind, and the soul and the spirit will go out and go on. *That* is the thing that matters, says the cross. The Lord is there because of the value he places upon the soul of man.

Another thing in this same connection is that obviously the most important thing for us, according to this preaching of the cross, is our relationship to God. We have dealt with man's relationship to man, and that is very important. But the message of the cross is that a man's relationship to his fellow man will never be right unless his relationship to God is put right first. And the cross keeps on saying that because everything depends upon it. Over and above everything else, here is the ultimate thing—where do I stand in my relationship to God? Why did the Son of God die on the cross? He will tell you. He came there because he wanted to restore men to the right relationship with God. God sent him to do that. 'God was in Christ, reconciling the world unto himself . . . .' He hath set him forth as 'a propitiation through faith in his blood'.

And then the next thing I find under this heading of exposition is that obviously the thing that makes sin sin, or, if you prefer it, *the very essence of sin, is rebellion against God*, the breaking of a relationship with God. That is the real meaning of sin. The world does not know it, but that is the great message of the cross. We tend to think of sin in terms of actions and bad acts, wrong things which we have done or thought, or wrong things which we have said. But that is not the serious thing about sin. The terrible thing about sin is that it is rebellion against God. It is man defying God. It is man breaking God's holy law. It is man trampling upon God's sanctities. It is man setting himself up, standing up to God, and defying God. That is the essence of sin. It is the most terrible thing a man can ever do for it means that he breaks the relationship with God and tries to set himself up as a god. The cross tells all that. It shows what a serious thing sin is. It is not just a question of actions which can be put right, so simply and so easily, by living a better life in the future. No, it is this question of relationship, the cross alone pinpoints that and emphasizes it. It brings this whole question of relationship with God to the very centre of my thinking.

And then it goes on to say that *there is a judgement upon sin, and that sin must be punished.* Now, listen to that cross, to the blood of the cross speaking to you, and this is what it says. It tells you that God is holy, and righteous, and just. You will find it all there in Romans 3:25, 26. And because God is who and what he is and because he is holy and righteous and just, he hates sin. His wrath is upon sin. Why did the Son of God ever die? He is the Son of God, he has never done any wrong. He has never broken his father's commandments. As we have seen nobody could point a finger at him, nobody could bring a charge against him which they could substantiate. Even the devil could not. And yet he dies. The cross answers the question. He dies upon the cross because God hates sin, and because God's holy wrath is upon sin. Sin cannot be trifled with by God, his holy nature prohibits it. Sin is the most serious matter that has ever entered into the whole universe.

Let me put it like this. The problem of sin is the greatest problem that even Almighty God has ever had to deal with. I

say that for this reason. Take the whole problem of creation.
Now, creation is a tremendous matter. There was nothing,
and God created. There at a certain point the Spirit broods
upon the abyss and the chaos, and God said: 'Let there be
light: and there was light.' God brought light into being by
the mere word of his power, his mere fiat. And God created
everything in the same way—a word was enough, such is
the power of God. He speaks and it is done.

But when God comes to deal with the problem of man,
and man in sin and rebellion, and man in alienation against
himself, a word is not enough. Had you realized this, have
you heard the cross preaching this? This is what the cross is
telling us. I say it with reverence, after due, deep consideration. I say it only on the authority of the Scripture. I say it
only because the cross preaches it. God cannot forgive sin
just by saying: 'I forgive.' If he could, he would have done so.
Do you imagine that God would ever have sent his only
begotten Son to the cross if he could have forgiven the sin of
men in any other way? Would God have abandoned his Son
to that, and poured out upon him the vials of his wrath?
Would he have allowed his only begotten, dearly beloved
Son, to cry out in agony, and to say, 'My God, my God, why
hast thou forsaken me?' while he endured the agony and the
thirst and the shame? Would he ever have allowed it if there
had been any other way? But there was not. A word is
enough to create, but a word is not enough to forgive. Before God can forgive any sin to any man, his only begotten
Son had to leave the courts of heaven, and come down on
earth and take on human nature, and live as a man and be
'stricken, smitten of God', upon that cross. And the cross
thus proclaims the holiness of God, the heinousness of sin,
the terrible problem of sin, the terrible seriousness of man's
rebellion against God.

So the question that I ask is not what sort of a life you are living. It is not that I am not interested, but that is not the first question. The question the Bible asks us all, the question that the cross puts to us, is not that, or how you spent last night; or whether you are moral or immoral; or what your thoughts are. No, its first question is: what is your relationship to God? God made man in his own image, so that he might live to his glory. The first great question in the shorter catechism of the Presbyterian Church, which I am never tired of quoting, is 'What is the chief end of man?' And here is the answer: 'The chief end of man is to glorify God, and to enjoy him forever.' God made us for that, and if you are not doing it, you are a terrible sinner. You say you have never committed adultery. I am not interested. You say you have never committed murder. That is not the first thing. The question is, are you living to the glory of God? Is God the chief end and object of your life? Is God the centre of your interest? Are you submitting yourself in obedience to him? *That* is the question.

That ultimately is the only question. The command that comes to you and to me is this: 'Thou shalt love the Lord thy God with all thy heart and with all thy soul, and with all thy mind, and with all thy strength' (Mk 12:30). And nothing less than that is of any interest to God. All your little respectability, and all your nice religiosity, is worthless, filthy rags, abomination, in the sight of God. He wants you, he wants your heart, he wants your allegiance, he wants the centre of your life. He will be content with nothing else. The cross, the blood of the cross, speaks all that. It was because man had come short of that, that he died on the cross. So it expounds all this to us, it unfurls it, it preaches it to us. That is what it is saying. We must listen to the cross. Do not sentimentalize it away with your superficiality. Oh, look at it and ask what it means. Listen to what it tells you, and to the exposition that one finds in the cross. That is what the blood of sprinkling speaks to us today.

But let me move to a second section. The cross, thank God, is not only exposition. The cross is also proclamation, a mighty declaration. I like the word that the Apostle uses there in Romans 3, and especially the way in which he repeats it. He likes it himself, obviously: 'Whom God hath set forth,' he says, 'to be a propitiation through faith in his blood, to declare his righteousness for the remission of sins that are past, through the forbearance of God; to declare, I say . . .' (Rom 3:25). Have you got it, have you heard it, were you listening? says the Apostle. Wake up, you sleepy listeners: '. . . to declare, I say . . . .' Have you heard the declaration? Have you heard the mighty proclamation? What does this blood declare to me? Let me sum it up in another word that this same Apostle used in 2 Corinthians 5:19, 21. This is the declaration: 'God was in Christ, reconciling the world unto himself, not imputing their trespasses unto them . . . . For he hath made him to be sin for us, who knew no sin, that we might be made the righteousness of God in him.' What does all this mean? Let me put it like this in modern terms. The cross tells me that this is the declaration. This, it says, is God's way of dealing with the problem of man's sin. It has already said that there is a problem. It is a terrible one, it is the greatest problem of the whole of history, of all time, and of the whole cosmos. There is nothing greater than this. There is the exposition of the problem. Then comes the mighty declaration. This, it says, is God's answer.

Now our Lord had been saying that in his teaching, but they could not understand it. They were blinded, even his own disciples. They were thinking as Jews, in terms of a kingdom on earth. Man will always materialize the great and glorious blessings of God's kingdom. When is the kingdom going to come? That was their question to him even after the resurrection, you remember. They did not understand what he had been telling them—that he had really come in order to die. 'The Son of Man,' he says, 'came not to be ministered unto, but to minister, and to give his life a ransom for many' (Mt 20:28). They could not take it. And there on the cross he was saying it again, and still they did not understand. Some people felt sorry for him, others offered their sympathy, others jeered at him; none of them understood what was happening. But what he was saying, and what the blood says as you listen to it, is that this is God's way of solving the problem of man's sin. It is this tremendous declaration. Now the term is put there before us very clearly. 'Whom God,' it says, 'hath *set forth*.' It is an interesting term. God, it tells us was setting forth his Son on the cross as a propitiation. 'Set forth' is like putting an advertisement in the paper, putting in a great announcement, with a great heading—listen, look, harken, exclamation marks, I am telling you something—God hath set forth. And then there is that other term—*to declare*. The Apostle says we are ambassadors. The business of an ambassador is to bear messages, to take a message from his own sovereign to another country. Paul tells them that this is what he has been told to say, and in the same way preachers are ambassadors for Christ, 'beseeching you in his stead'. These are the terms, and the cross, therefore, is a public declaration. It is an historic event. It is not an idea, or a theory, the cross is something that happened on a cross, on a hill called Calvary, nearly 2000 years ago. Historic, public, evident, visible, the whole world knows about it. God has set it forth. He has made a pronouncement, and called attention to it.

And what is he saying? Now this is how the Apostle puts it in Romans 3. It is a most amazing thing. God has to justify himself for forgiving. Had you ever thought of that? This shows you the problem of forgiveness. The trouble with all of us is that we do not know God. We think in sentimental terms. Our whole notion of love is so abased, so unworthy, that we do not know what love means. Still less do we know what holiness means. But, according to the Apostle, this is something that God has got to do, he must justify himself for forgiving. He has set his Son forth 'to be a propitiation through faith in his blood, to declare his righteousness for the remission of sins that are past, through the forbearance of God.' Had you ever considered this problem? How can a holy God forgive? How can a God who says that he is going to punish sin, forgive sin? But he had been forgiving the children of Israel under the Old Testament dispensation. They had often repented and had come back to him, and God had forgiven them. How does God justify himself in forgiving the sins of the children of Israel throughout the whole Old Testament period? How can he do that? How can God remain just and absolutely holy and at the same time forgive a sinner? And here he declares the answer. The cross is a mighty declaration. And what it says is this. The Son is a propitiation. In other words, God on the cross was punishing sin. He said that he would, and he has done it.

God has always said that sin is to be punished, that his holy wrath is upon it, and that he cannot deal with sin in any other terms. And he has done exactly what he promised. On the cross he is doing it publicly. There he is, once and for all, at the central point of history, pouring out his wrath upon the sins of man in the body of his own Son. He is striking him, he is smiting him, he is condemning him to death. He dies, and his blood speaks. It is God's punishment of sin and evil. It is a mighty declaration that God has done what he has always said he would do, namely, that he would punish sin, and the wages of sin is death. And there you see it happening upon the cross. It is an announcement, a proclamation, that this is God's way of dealing with the problem of sin. I hasten to say this. It is obviously the only way to deal with sin, and the cross says that.

> There was no other good enough
>   To pay the price of sin;
> He only could unlock the gate
>   Of heaven and let us in.

Mrs C. F. Alexander

It is not surprising that the gospel of the cross and the blood of Christ has produced some of the greatest poetry that the world has ever known. We sing at Christmas time:

> Hark! the herald angels sing
> Glory to the new-born King;
> Peace on earth, and mercy mild,
> God and sinners reconciled.

C. Wesley

That is what has happened. God and sinners reconciled! It was the only way whereby it could be done, it is the announcement and the proclamation that it has been done.

But I cannot leave things here without giving you my third division. The cross as a sermon, the blood of Christ speaking, is not only exposition and declaration and pronouncement. Blessed be the name of God, it is also invitation: '... the blood of sprinkling, that speaketh better things than that of Abel'. Abel's blood has no invitation in it. Abel's blood cries out for retribution, for punishment, there is no invitation there to anybody, except to the wrath of a holy God. But in this other blood 'that speaketh better things than that of Abel', there is a word of invitation. And from your standpoint and mine, now looking at it very practically, there is nothing more wonderful about the cross than just this. We have seen that the cross is an event. The cross is an historical event. It is a setting forth in public of this great act of God. But thank God it does not stop there. It is an appeal, it is an invitation, it asks us to listen as we value our own immortal souls. You know the Old Testament prophets had seen something of this. They had not seen it very clearly. They were not meant to, and they could not see so far off. They saw something of the sufferings of Christ and the glory that was to follow, but they had not seen this. One of them, at the height of his prophetic inspiration, put what he saw into the mouth of the Messiah that was to come, when he said, 'Look unto me, and be ye saved, all the ends of the earth' (Is 45:22). 'Look unto me.' It is an invitation. That is not only proclamation, that is an invitation. Look unto me!

And you remember how our blessed Lord himself uses similar language. These are his words: 'Come unto me, all ye that labour and are heavy laden, and I will give you rest' (Mt 11:28). Come, invitation. Oh there are tremendous things there. You listen to the preaching of the blood of Christ, and you are terrified, and alarmed. You see your utter hopelessness. But wait, he has not finished. Come, there is an invitation. I like the way the apostle Paul puts it in Ephesians 2. It is so wonderful. I would urge you to read it again. He says: 'For he is our peace, who hath made both one, and hath broken down the middle wall of partition between us; having abolished in his flesh the enmity, even the law of commandments contained in ordinances; for to make in himself of twain one new man, so making peace; and that he might reconcile both unto God in one body by the cross, having slain the enmity thereby:' but go on: 'and came and preached peace to you which were afar off, and to them that were nigh' (vv. 14–17). He preached peace by the blood of his cross. By dying upon the cross, he is preaching peace.

But he is preaching peace to them which are afar off as well as to them that are nigh. This is the thing I want to emphasize because it is one of the most glorious things about the cross. To whom is this invitation given? To whom does the cross, the blood of sprinkling, cry out today saying,

'Come'? Listen, it is to them that are afar off. Not to the Jews, the religious people only, but also to the Gentiles, the dogs, those outside the law. Strangers from the commonwealth of Israel. Those who did not know these things, it is to them, who are afar off, as well as to them that are nigh. Oh, there is nothing more wonderful about the gospel than the way our Lord said such things as this: 'They that are whole have no need of the physician, but they that are sick: I came not to call the righteous, but sinners to repentance' (Mk 2:17)— these are the people he has come for, to whom he gives this invitation. This is, I say, one of the most glorious aspects of all in connection with this cross. This is where the cross is unique. The cross, the blood of sprinkling, speaks in our day to people to whom nothing else in the whole universe speaks.

What do you mean, says someone? Let me explain. To whom does philosophy speak? Take your great text books on philosophy; to whom do they speak? Do they speak to you, can you follow them? To whom does the atheistic phil-osopher speak? He speaks only to the 'wise', he speaks only to those who have got brains and understanding, who can follow his reason and his logic and his terminology. He does not speak to anyone else. To whom do morality and ethics speak? These men are concerned about the good life, they say they are concerned about the moral state of this country, and they address their moral and their ethical appeals to us. To whom do they speak? They only speak to people who are already good. They have nothing to say to the bad. They only speak to those who are strong willed, and to those who are interested in ethics and morality.

They have nothing to say to anyone else. Let me continue with something that some of you may wonder at. To whom does religion speak? I did not say Christianity, I said religion. And when I say religion I mean just church or chapel-going, I mean merely attending a place of worship and perhaps being active in it, and being proud of your denomination, and very interested in these matters and that is all. That is what I mean by religion. To whom does religion speak? It only speaks to a handful of its devotees, and it does not speak to anyone else. It does not speak to people who are not interested in those things. But here is a message that speaks to all. Thank God for 'the blood of sprinkling, that speaketh better things than that of Abel'. Here is a blood that speaks to people to whom nothing else speaks.

But we see that this blood gives its invitation only to certain people. Indeed, there are some people to whom the blood of sprinkling does not speak better things than that of Abel. Who are they? Oh, they are the 'clever' people, it has no invitation for them; the self-righteous, it has no invitation for them; the self-satisfied, it has no invitation for them. If you come to him standing erect upon your feet, proud of your knowledge and your learning, glorying in the fact that you are a twentieth century man, and that you are good and moral, and an idealist who wants to put an end to war. If you think you can uplift the human race by your own efforts—if you come like that, this gospel has no invitation for you, the blood of sprinkling will condemn you. It will show you to yourself for what you are, as we have already seen. It will show you that all your righteousness is but as filthy rags, it will humble you, it will condemn you, it will abase you to the ground, it will cast you to the dust. There will be no invitation to you.

But thank God, if you are already grovelling in the dust, if you are afar off, then it speaks to you, its invitation is to you. To whom does the invitation of this cross come? It comes to the failures, the people who know they have gone wrong, the people who are filled with a sense of shame, the people who are weary and tired and forlorn in the struggle. Oh, I have already quoted—'Come unto me, all ye that labour and are heavy laden, and I will give you rest.' And you know he is talking about people who are labouring to live a good and a clean and a straight life. That is what he means by labouring and being heavy laden—the law of God, the Commandments, moral ideals. You have tried and have sweated and fasted. You are labouring, like Martin Luther before he saw the truth, like John Wesley before he saw it. Like all these people before they saw it, labouring, trying to live the good life, but failing; miserable failures, weary and forlorn.

The hymns of the church have always expressed this.

> I heard the voice of Jesus say,
>   'Behold, I freely give
> The living water, thirsty one;
>   Stoop down, and drink, and live:'
>
> I came to Jesus as I was,
>   Weary, and worn, and sad;
>
> *H. Bonar*

That is how they have come. The invitation is to such. Weary, worn. Have you been engaged in this moral struggle? Do you feel that you are a failure, that the whole thing is hopeless? Do you despise yourself, kick yourself metaphorically, and feel you are no good? Weary, forlorn, tired, and on top of it all, sad and miserable? Nothing can comfort you. The pleasures of the world mock you. They do not give you anything. Life has disappointed you, and you are sad, miserable and unhappy, and on top of it all, you have a sense of guilt within you. Your conscience nags at you, condemns, raises up your past and puts it before you, and you know that you are unworthy, you know that you are a failure, you know that there is no excuse, you are guilty. But still worse, you know that you are unclean, you know that your heart is unclean. For it is out of the heart that come evil thoughts, murders, adulteries, fornications, and all the rest. The heart is the trouble, and you have come to see that you are rotten, that in you there is no good thing. Oh wretched man, you say, who shall deliver me? Here you are, not only guilty, but you are unclean, you are vile, you are foul. 'Foul, I to the fountain fly', says another hymn. The writer has seen it, he has felt it, he has known it.

And then on top of all this, you are filled with a sense of fear. You are afraid of life, you are afraid of yourself and your own weakness, you are afraid of tomorrow. You are afraid of death, you know it is coming and you can do nothing about it, but you are afraid of it. Oh, what lies beyond it? Thoughts come to you of that 'unknown bourne from which no travel-ler returns'. Death is coming, and there you are, you can do nothing, and you feel guilty and you are full of fear of God, the judgement, and hell, and terror and alarm possess you. You feel utterly hopeless and completely helpless. You have tried so often, only to fail. You have made your resolutions but you have never kept them, you have had good and noble ideas, but you have never put them into practice. You have tried, you have fasted, you have sweated, you have prayed, you have read, you have done everything, but the more you do, the more vile you see yourself, and the more hopeless. You say to yourself, I am no good, I am damned, I am lost, I am unworthy, I am a mass of pollution. 'Oh, wretched man that I am!' 'In me (that is in my flesh) dwelleth no good thing' (Rom 7:24, 18).

And this is the amazing thing about the cross. It comes to such a person, and it is to such a person above all others that it brings its gracious and its glorious invitation. What does it say to you? I am not speaking to self-satisfied, self-righteous persons at this moment, I have already spoken to you, and I trust that you have seen yourself in all the horror of your self-deception. I am speaking to those who are on the ground, grovelling in their utter helplessness, and with a guilt and a sense of uncleanness and shame, having lost their chastity, their purity, their morality, their everything. To anyone like that, I would say, You are afar off, and the cross speaks to you with sympathy. That man dying on that cross was known as the friend of publicans and sinners. He was reviled by the good and the religious because he sat down and ate meat and drank with publicans and sinners. He had sympathy. There was a wild, demon possessed man, whom they could not tame and could not hold, even by chains and fetters, but the moment he saw the Lord he came running to him. So did they all. He had sympathy.

Not only that, he will tell you that he is ready to accept you. The world picks up its skirt and passes by. It leaves you alone, it does not want to associate with you, you have gone down, you belong to the refuse and the gutters, and the world is too respectable to have any interest in you. Here is one who is ready to receive you and to accept you. Here is one above all you gives you rest. 'Come unto me, all ye that labour and are heavy laden, and I will give you rest.' An end to this vain, futile, useless struggle. Sit down, he says, and listen, the blood of sprinkling is speaking. Wait, stop, give up your activities. Just as you are, I am ready to receive you. In your rags, in your filth, in your vileness. Rest.

What else? Pardon. The cross speaks of benediction, of pardon, joy and peace with God. It tells you that God is ready to forgive you, the blood of sprinkling tells you that. It says, listen to me, your sin has been punished. I am here because this is the punishment of sin. Listen to me, says the blood of sprinkling, I have been shed that you might be forgiven, pardoned, at peace with God. Oh, thank God, there is also cleansing here. When you feel your vileness and see the blemishes and spots of iniquity upon you, you learn that:

> There is a fountain filled with blood,
> Drawn from Emmanuel's veins,

And sinners plunged beneath that flood.
Lose all their guilty stains.

The dying thief rejoiced to see
That fountain in his day;
And there have I, as vile as he,
Washed all my sins away.

W. Cowper

That is what the blood of sprinkling says. So it tells you that out of your very misery you can have joy, beauty for ashes. It will give you a new nature, it tells you. It will give you a new start in life. It will give you a new power and a strength to resist everything that has got you down, and it will give you an everlasting and an eternal hope. The blood of sprinkling says that the Son of God has borne all your punishment, that everything that stood between God and forgiving you has been removed. That God forgives you everything freely and immediately.

Let not conscience make you linger,
Nor of fitness fondly dream;
All the fitness He requireth,
Is to feel your need of Him.
This he gives you;
'Tis the Spirit's rising beam.

J. Hart

The cross announces a free gift of pardon and forgiveness, reconciliation and restoration and all you need; new life in Christ and an eternal hope, and all at once. And it all comes from this blessed person, whose body was broken and whose blood began to flow, on the cross. He is inviting you, he is calling to you. Do you hear him, are you ready?

But oh, says someone, you have no idea what I am like, you have no idea what I have done, you have no idea what I

have been. But my dear friend, you are not the first to have
said that. A man wrote a hymn, we often sing it, and he puts
it like this:

> If I ask Him to receive me,
>   Will He say me nay?

Will he really receive me if I ask him to receive me, or will
he say me nay? This is the answer:

> 'Not till earth and not till heaven
>   Pass away.'

Again you ask:

> Finding, following, keeping, struggling,
>   Is He sure to bless?

Here again is the answer:

> 'Saints, apostles, prophets, martyrs,
>   Answer, "Yes".'

Stephen of Saba

Some of the greatest saints the church has ever known
were once vile, foul sinners, but they heard the invitation
coming from the blood of sprinkling, they believed it, and
they found it to be true. So finding, following, keeping, struggling, is he sure to bless? Here is the answer. Not only does
the word say it, not only does the blood say it, the saints of
the centuries say it: 'Saints, apostles, prophets, martyrs,
answer, "yes".' Trust him. He has never broken his word, he
has never forfeited or gone back upon his promise. Believe,
they say, the blood of sprinkling, and you will find it to be
true. So I ask you to join with the hymn writer in saying:

> I hear thy welcome voice,
> That calls me, Lord, to thee,
> For cleansing in thy precious Blood
> That flowed on Calvary.

I am coming, Lord!
Coming now to thee!
Wash me, cleanse me, in the Blood
That flowed on Calvary.

L. Hartsough

Do that and you will find it to be true.

Chapter 8

A New Nature

We would almost think at this stage that we have seen all the glories which Paul saw in the cross, but that is not so—their number is not exhausted, there is more for us to see, as the Apostle still goes on glorying in it. He does so because it is to him the source and the centre out of which, and from which, come all the blessings that he has ever enjoyed as a Christian man. Now this is the thing I want to emphasize at this point. There is nothing ultimately possible for us in the way of good, apart from the cross. The cross is the source, the origin, and the centre of every blessing. There is no Christian blessing possible to anyone apart from the cross. It is impossible for anyone to be blessed by God in any way ultimately, apart from the cross. The cross is the key that opens, if I may so put it, the heart of God. And without the cross we know no blessings at all. This is a most important point. Why did the Apostle not say: 'God forbid that I should glory, save in the teaching of the Lord Jesus Christ'? Now that is what some of us would like him to say, is it not? That is what the modern man would like him to say. The modern man admires the Sermon on the Mount. He says that that is what we need, that there is the most wonderful ethical, moral, standard that has ever been invented and thought of by man, and that is what we want. There are many people who are not Christians who praise the Sermon on the Mount. The late Mr Gandhi, who died a Hindu, praised it. And there are many others who do the same. There are many infidels today who praise the Sermon on the Mount. They like Jesus, the teacher, the religious teacher, the political agitator, as they regard him, and they are ready to laud his teaching in the Sermon on the Mount. They say that is the very thing the world needs. If only everybody practised that, all our problems would be solved.

Why does the Apostle not say, therefore, 'God forbid that I should glory, save in the Sermon on the Mount? God forbid that I should glory, save in the teaching, the incomparable teaching, of the Son of God'? There is, as we have seen, a perfectly simple and obvious answer to this question. It is not the teaching of the Son of God that saves us. Indeed we can say this with reverence—the actual teaching of the Lord Jesus Christ was a failure, a complete failure. His teaching did not reform anybody. His teaching did not even penetrate into the minds and the hearts of his own chosen disciples. They stumbled. Read the gospel. You find that they stumbled, especially when he talked about his death. They could not take it. But look at it like this. Take the Sermon on the Mount that people praise so much. Where is the man who can live and practise the Sermon on the Mount? There is all the difference in the world between praising the Sermon on the Mount and practising it. There is all the difference in the world between applauding it and applying it. It is impossible for man to keep the Sermon on the Mount in his own strength. Man cannot even keep the Ten Commandments. And yet he talks glibly about keeping the Sermon on the Mount, and of imitating Christ. We have shown how there is nothing that so condemns us as the Sermon on the Mount, and the life of the Lord Jesus Christ.

The Jews were a race of people to whom God had already given his law through his servant Moses, and they could not keep it. They could not keep the Ten Commandments. Nobody has ever kept them perfectly, because the Ten Commandments includes this sentence: 'Thou shalt not covet', which means that thou shalt not desire. And if man cannot keep the Ten Commandments as they understand them, what hope have they of keeping the Ten Commandments as they have been interpreted by the Lord Jesus Christ?

That was the whole trouble with the Pharisees, who so hated him and who finally crucified him. They thought that they were keeping the Ten Commandments and the moral law. Our Lord convinced them and convicted them of the fact that they were not doing so. They claimed that they had never committed murder. Wait a minute, said our Lord. Have you ever said to your brother, 'Thou fool'? If you have, you are guilty of murder. Murder does not only mean actually, physically, killing a man, it means that bitterness and hatred in your heart. You say, 'You fool'—and you are really killing him with your mouth. And you are guilty of murder. And he taught the same, you remember, with regard to adultery. They claimed that they were guiltless. But wait a minute, says our Lord, you say you have never committed adultery? 'But I say unto you, that whosoever looketh on a woman to lust after her, hath committed adultery with her already in his heart' (Mt 5:28). He is guilty. He has coveted; he has desired. You see, as our Lord comes to interpret the law, he shows that an evil desire is as damnable as a deed. And a thought and an imagination are as reprehensible in the sight of God as the act committed. So nobody can keep the Sermon on the Mount.

And that is why the Apostle does not say: 'God forbid that I should glory, save in the Sermon on the Mount, or in the teaching of the Lord Jesus Christ.' The teaching of Christ condemned everybody, the Pharisees included, and showed everybody to be a complete and entire and hopeless failure. So you do not glory in that. No, Paul glories in the cross, because it is through and from the cross that everything becomes possible, and all the blessings of the Christian life are laid open before us. The cross is the door that leads to all blessings. Without it there is nothing. Without the cross and all it means, we have no blessings from God at all. But the cross opens the possibility to all of the endless blessings of the glorious God.

What are they? Let me note some of them to you here. The Apostle Paul never got tired of saying these things. Read what he says at the beginning of Romans. He puts it like this: 'Therefore being justified by faith, we have peace with God through our Lord Jesus Christ' (Rom 5:1). Justified by faith means that the moment you believe in what happened on the cross, and see that that is God's way of reconciling you unto himself, you are immediately regarded as just, your sins are all forgiven and blotted out, and you are clothed in the righteousness of Christ. 'Therefore,' says Paul, 'being justified by faith we have peace with God.' That is the first thing that comes out of this belief. Now, I have often said, and I say it again now, that there is no more important word, especially in these letters of the apostle Paul than the word *therefore*. Note it. He always brings this word 'therefore' in at a point of this kind. He has been laying down the doctrine, and especially the doctrine of the cross, and then he says, 'therefore'—in the light of that, because of that, this is what follows.

And here is the first thing that follows. Being justified by faith we have peace with God. Do you realize what that means? Do you realize that that is the most important and the most wonderful thing that can ever happen to you, that you are given peace and made at peace with God? We have shown how all our troubles in this life as human beings are due to the fact that we are in the wrong relationship to God. It is as simple as that. All the varied and complicated problems of the human race today, as they have always been throughout the running centuries, all emanate from just one thing, that man is in the wrong relationship to God. He is alienated from God. There is a state of warfare between man and God. That is the cause of all our troubles. Trouble came into this world as the direct and immediate result of man's rebellion against God, and it has continued ever since.

And we have tried so much, and civilization has been so busy in trying to bring order into the chaos, in trying to arrive at peace. Everybody wants peace—but do what we may, we cannot find it. Why not? Because we will never find it until we are at peace with God. God himself said it through the prophet Isaiah: 'There is no peace, saith my God, to the wicked' (57:21), and if ever the world were proving that, it is proving it today. It does not matter how much money you have, or how much learning, how much understanding, how much influence, or how much power, you will never know peace while you are wicked, which means while you are not subservient to God and living to his glory and to his praise. You can have all the money and the wealth of the greatest millionaire in the world, but you can be as restless and as unhappy as the poorest pauper.

'There is no peace, saith my God, to the wicked.' And there is no hope for man until he arrives at peace with God. Why is this so important? Well the answer is, of course, that we are in the hands of God, whether we like it or not. Let me put it like this. Here is the position of man as he is by nature. Here is the position of every man and woman who is not a Christian, who does not believe in the cross of Christ, and does not glory in it. As we are by nature, God is displeased with us, and his wrath is upon us. He is displeased with us because he has made us, and he made us with a given end and object in view. But we are not fulfilling that. We are not living and behaving as he intended us to. And so God is displeased with us.

Now it is inevitable that God should be displeased. The great Almighty God in all his wisdom and justice and love and compassion, who made this world and all men and women, never made the world that you and I know today. The thing is monstrous. The world as you and I see it and know it is not God's world as he made it. It is what man has made of God's world that you and I are familiar with. And that is not well pleasing to God. He made everything at the beginning. He made it perfect, and we are told that he looked at his creation and he saw that it was good. He was pleased with it. But God is displeased with the world as it is today, and he has said so repeatedly. His wrath is upon it, and he is determined to punish it, and more than that, he is punishing it.

There is a great argument in the New Testament. This is not the place to develop it, though it seems to me to be vitally important at this present juncture in the history of the human race. But there is an argument to this effect, that God manifests his wrath against the sin of man by just allowing man to reap the consequences of his own actions. God does not always punish directly, he sometimes punishes indirectly. We have all done it with somebody else at some time or another. You may be trying to persuade a child to behave and to do things in the right way. You know that if the child puts its finger on some little electric machine, that it is going to get a shock. But the very fact that you tell the child not to touch that machine makes the child want to touch it more and more. You may keep on saying to the child: 'Do not touch it, or you'll be sorry', but the child is determined. 'All right then,' you say, and you pretend you are not looking. So the little rebel puts his finger on it and gets the electric shock. God does that with mankind.

I believe that explains this present century, with its two world wars, and all the present chaos and confusion. God is saying to man: You have said that you can get on without me. Very well, get on without me. But do not expect people to be loyal to their marriage vows, do not expect them not to fight and not to build up armaments. They will not listen, because once they have left me, they are governed by their own lusts and passions and desires, and reap the consequences. That is what is happening in the modern world, the wrath of God is upon it. God is not smiling upon the world today, or blessing it. The world hates him and rebels against him and blasphemes him, and God withdraws his own blessings. You are seeing a world unblessed by God. That is the wrath of God.

But there is another side. Look at it from man's side. Man by nature, man without God, is restless. We know that, every one of us, everybody is restless. It is one of the greatest problems in life, is it not? Oh, how to find peace. Where can we find peace? Where can we find tranquillity? Where can we find rest and peace of mind and of heart and of spirit? Where can we find the point, where all is well and nothing troubles? Where is it? Man cannot find it, he is restless. Why? I have already been giving you the answer. Man, though he does not know it, was made by God, and he was made in such a way that he is dependent upon God. There is the highest thing in man which can only be satisfied by God. Nothing else can satisfy it.

Now man has tried to find satisfaction elsewhere. Read the book of Ecclesiastes in the Old Testament, and there you will see the whole thing laid out before you. Man tries to find satisfaction in wealth, in dancing, in drinking, in women and wine. He tries everything, but he cannot find peace. It is impossible. Man is too big for that. Some people have thought that if you give a man a new house, it will make him perfectly happy. They say, 'What we want is a housing scheme.' 'Education,' says another. We have tried them all. Man still cannot find peace. We are better housed that we have ever been, we are better educated, better everything, but there is no peace. Man is still restless. Why? Because he is too big. You do not change a man by changing his house, or by giving him a little more knowledge and information and education. The man remains the same. Yes—'The rank is but the guinea's stamp; . . . A man's a man for a' that.'

Of course he is. It does not matter what his title is; it does not matter what his clothes are like. A man's a man for all that, and he is restless, he is not at peace, because, I say, he has been made in such a way that he can only get peace when he conforms to the laws of his own being and his own nature. And he does not do that. He does not want to do it, and he is restless, he is dissatisfied. He hates the notion of God, and at the same time he is filled with fear. He is afraid of the unknown. He is afraid of ill-health. He is afraid of death. He is afraid of that unknown bourne from which no traveller returns. He spends his time in fear. He says, of course, that he is not afraid. He pretends he is not, but he is, he is restless, and he is unhappy. Why should he be afraid of all these things? There is only one adequate answer, the Bible has it. 'The sting of death is sin; and the strength of sin is the law' (1 Cor 15:56). Man, though he denies God, has a guilt complex, he feels guilty. He cannot get rid of it. His psychologists have got it themselves. They cannot explain it away, and they suffer from it in their own lives. Man has a sense of guilt. Though he does not believe in God, he still has the sense of guilt in the presence of God.

Before man can ever know peace, and, in particular, peace with God, the two sides must be dealt with. Man is at enmity with God, and God's wrath is upon man. Something has to happen on God's side, and the message of the cross is that that has happened. When our Lord died upon the cross he was fulfilling every demand of God's holy law. The righteousness and the justice and the holiness of God were fully satisfied. God poured out his wrath upon sin in the body of his own Son. His soul was made an offering for sin, and all the demands of God in his holiness were satisfied there. And, thank God, it works on our side also. We have a feeling that God is against us. We think of God as some great ogre, or monster, waiting to pounce upon us and to punish us; we feel that he hates us and that he is against us, and spoiling our lives. We do not want to be bothered by him, and want to go our own way.

Then the moment comes when we look at that cross, and see that God sent his only begotten, dearly beloved Son into this world in order that he might go to the cross. It was God who sent him to it. 'God was in Christ, reconciling the world unto himself . . . .' It was God who 'laid on him the iniquity of us all'. It is God who smote him and struck him and gave him the punishment that we deserved. As you look at the cross, I say again, your whole attitude towards God, and our whole opinion of God, changes completely. There we see that God is love and full of mercy and of compassion; that God loves us with an everlasting love. So you see that by the cross, God's wrath is satisfied and appeased, and our folly and our rebellion are taken away, and God and man are brought together, and our peace is made with God.

The great Saint Augustine of Hippo has put it all in a memorable phrase: 'Thou hast made us for thyself, and our hearts are restless until they find their rest in thee.' Man can find peace, but he only finds it when he is put at peace with God. It is only by the death of Christ on the cross that the warfare and the rebellion and the antagonism and the wrath of God are all dealt with, and all is removed. And God looks down upon us in loving compassion and forgiveness and smiles upon us, 'Being justified by faith, we have peace with God.'

There, then, is the first thing, but let me hurry on. There are many other things that proceed from this cross. I start with the peace because it is the most important of them all. But let me now say just a word or two about the second thing. I do not mean to be insulting when I put this question to you. Can you follow? Can you understand that portion of scripture which you find in chapter 5 of Romans and the first half of chapter 6. Those words were written, just over 1900 years ago, to the Christian people in Rome, and most of them were slaves or servants in Caesar's household. And when Paul wrote those words to them, he obviously meant them to understand them, and he assumed that they would. But I am asking you twentieth century men and women who are proud of your learning and of your knowledge and sophistication—do you understand them? First century serfs and slaves could understand this. Can we? This is what Paul said. He said that we should glory in the cross because when the Son of God died upon that cross, all who believe in him, died with him. 'Knowing this,' says Romans 6:6, 'that our old man is crucified with him.' He says: 'For if we have been planted together in the likeness of his death, we shall be also in the likeness of his resurrection' (6:5). What does all this mean?

Let me try to explain it. The great argument of the Apostle there in that portion of scripture beginning at Romans 5:12 and going on almost to the beginning of Romans 8, is just this: the most important thing that we can ever understand about ourselves in this world is our position, and that is that we are, all of us, the descendants of Adam. God created a man, he called him Adam, and everybody has come out of that first man and the first woman, Eve. And the explanation of the state of the world is that we are all involved in that original fall and sin of Adam and Eve. Some of you, I know, do not believe that. Can you explain the universality of sin apart from that? Can you explain, in any way except this, the human race as it is, in spite of all the efforts of civilization to improve it? There is no other explanation. You see it is like this. Adam was our representative. He was the first of the human race, and God made him the representative of the human race, so that everything that he did involves the whole of his posterity. And we know well what happened. He sinned, and he fell, and he died, and the Apostle says that because of that we all died: 'Therefore, as through one man sin entered into the world, and death through sin; and so death passed unto all men, for that all sinned' (Rom 5:12 RV).

We were all involved in that act of Adam. We were all, as it were, in Adam. Adam was the head and the representative and the focus of the whole of humanity, and when he fell, we all fell with him. The punishment of sin is death. He died, we have all died ever since. Everybody, he says, dies. Even children die. Death came into the world and all die as the result of the sin of Adam. All the consequences of his sin and fall have fallen upon the whole of the human race. We are born with corrupted minds; we are born with perverted minds; we are born sinners. We try to toy with imaginary thought, in order to make ourselves feel happy for a while. We indulge in our fancies and fantasies, we paint our pictures with our imaginations, but they are not true. There is no such thing as an innocent babe. The first thing we all want to do is something that we are told not to do. We have all been born the children of Adam, and we are in him and tied to him, and there we all are by nature. He was miserable after he fell, and we have been miserable ever since, and we can do nothing about it.

And then comes the message of the gospel. Christ, who is he? He is the Son of God. But why did he come on earth? He came on earth to start a new humanity. He is the second Adam, he is the second man. The first man was Adam; the second man is the Lord Jesus Christ. 'The first man is of the earth, earthy: the second man is the Lord from heaven' (1 Cor 15:48).

Here, then, is this wonderful thing, that if you believe in the Lord Jesus Christ he becomes your representative. And everything that he did, he did for you, so that you have done it in him. We all fell in Adam, argues Paul. We can all be raised in Christ. And if you believe in him, it means that you have died with him, you have borne your punishment, you have finished with that old man that you once were. You no longer belong to Adam, you belong to Christ. You have a new start, a new beginning, and a new nature. You are in Christ, and no longer in Adam. This is a tremendous thing, so tremendous that none of us can understand it, and those of us who have known it for many years feel that we are only at the beginning of it, and this is the most wonderful thing of all.

You see, this is where the glory of the gospel comes in. 'Can the Ethiopian change his skin, or the leopard his spots?' The world says no—what a man is, so he remains. You cannot start afresh, you cannot have a new beginning. You will always be what you were. It is no use pretending, it cannot be done. Man is what he is and will remain what he is. No, says the gospel. It *is* possible for a man to become dead to what he was. He can cease to belong to Adam. He can cease to be in Adam; he can be in Christ. He can have undergone a death. He can have an entirely new birth, a new start, a new nature, a new life. He dies with Christ; he rises with Christ. He is in Christ. And so he becomes a new man.

Now, this is, of course, the very thing that had happened to the apostle Paul. In his old life he was a self-satisfied, proud Pharisee, a religious and highly moral man; a very good man, and a very nationalistic Jew, despising everybody else and proud of himself. That is what he was, and yet he was miserable and wretched and unhappy and disturbed. But once he realized the meaning of the death of the Lord Jesus Christ on the cross, he made an absolutely new start. Saul of Tarsus died, and the apostle Paul began to live. He says 'If any man be in Christ, he is a new creature: old things are passed away; behold, all things are become new' (2 Cor 5:17). He is a new man in a new universe. He is delivered from that old Adamic state and nature and he is in Christ, alive unto God. It is the cross that does that. There is nothing that will get rid of the old man that we all are by nature, but the death on the cross. But if you believe in him and in the purpose of that death, and what that death accomplished, you are truly dead to your old Adamic nature. You know that your old man was crucified with Christ, and that he has gone, and that he has gone forever. And as a result of this, our whole position and status is entirely changed. The Apostle put that in this great statement: 'For sin shall not have dominion over you: for ye are not under the law, but under grace' (Rom 6:14).

Oh, that men and women might understand what that means. You know, people will think of Christianity as just that which offers pardon for our sin, that God says: 'Very well, I forgive', but that then you remain exactly where you were, and you go back into the same old world with your same old weakness. And there you are as you always were, and you fail and you sin again, and you ask forgiveness again, and up and down you go, back and forth, and you are exactly the same, except that now God forgives you when you forgive him. But that is not Christianity. That may be the beginning of it, and the essential beginning of it, but it is nothing but the beginning. This is the essential thing—that my whole position is changed, my whole relationship to God is changed. I am not only at peace with him, I am in an entirely new relationship. This is the difference.

'Ye,' says the Apostle, 'are not under the law, but under grace' (Rom 6:15), by which he means that all of us by nature are under law, under the law of God. If you are not reconciled to God, if you do not believe in Christ and his death upon the cross, if you are not a forgiven person because of that belief, I will tell you exactly what your position is. You are under the law of God. God deals with you as a law giver. He says, here are my Commandments, keep them. If you can keep them I will be satisfied. If you cannot, I will punish you. That is to be under the law. We are all under the law of England and that is the position. The law lays down its commandments. It says if you break them you will be prosecuted, and if you are found guilty, you will suffer the punishment that fits that particular crime. We are under law. And the whole of the human race, apart from Christ, is in that position of being under law.

And you know what the law of God demands of you? The Ten Commandments. Have no other God beside him; make no graven image of him; nor take his name in vain; nor take his day in vain. Thou shalt not kill. Thou shalt not steal. Thou shalt not commit adultery. Thou shalt not bear false witness, thou shalt not covet thy neighbour's wife or his ox or his ass or his man servant, or his maid servant. And there is much more. And then Christ sums it all up like this: 'Thou shalt love the Lord thy God with all thy heart, and all thy soul, and with all thy strength, and with all thy mind; and thy neighbour as thyself' (Lk 10:27).

That is the law of God, that is what you and I have got to keep by nature. God says there is my law, there is my demand, that is what I am going to judge you by, and if you do not keep it, I will punish you. That is being under law. There is the task for you. And it offers you no help whatsoever to keep it. Of course, you say you do not want help. You are confident in your will power, in your knowledge and your education, and your moralisms. You do not want help. Very well, you are not given any either, and that is the life you have got to live without any help. And the result is, of course, that you cannot do it. 'For what the law could not do, in that it was weak through the flesh,' says the Apostle. It is impossible. No man can keep the law of God, no man ever has kept it. The whole world lieth guilty before God, there is none righteous, no not one. All have sinned and come short of the glory of God.

So there you are, you are still under law. You cannot keep it, you are helpless, you are a failure, you are miserable, you are getting older, you are going to die, and after death you stand before God in the judgement and you can do nothing, and you are left in utter despair. That is what it means by being under law. And it is so hopeless that it makes many a man say, 'Very well, if I am already damned in any case, I am going to make the best of it. I am going to get my fill of sinning, while I am here!' It makes you sin all the more. And then the guilt comes all the more, and there you are in utter hopelessness and helplessness, under law.

But this cross, the cross of the Lord Jesus Christ, makes an entire change. You are not under law, he says, but under grace. You, who have believed in the Lord Jesus Christ and his death upon the cross, you have been taken from that position, you are in an entirely new position. You are under grace, and grace is unmerited favour. It is kindness shown to people who deserve nothing but punishment. Grace is God, because he is God, looking upon us with favour when we do not deserve anything at all. That is what 'under grace' means. It means that God is no longer just a law-giver to you, he is your Father. He is your Father who loves you with an everlasting love. He is your Father who looks upon you and desires to bless you. He is one who says, 'You are my child, I am your Father, I will give you my own nature. I will count the very hairs of your head. I will number them all. Nothing shall happen to you apart from me.' That is to be under grace.

You see the difference? It is the difference between being in a relationship of law and a relationship of love. You are in an entirely new position and the cross puts you there. You are under grace, and you do not tremble before God with a craven fear. You know that though you are unworthy, he is your Father, and you say, 'My Father, who art in heaven, hallowed be thy name, thy kingdom come.' And you know that he looks upon you with a smile. You know that he is patient, that he is long-suffering. You know that he is determined to bring you back to the perfection in which he originally made you, and that all the forces of his love and grace and compassion are working in your favour.

Let me put my last point to you in this form. It is that the cross entirely transforms the whole problem of life and living in this world, while we are still left in it, and it does it in this way. You believe in the Son of God and his death upon the cross, and God will put his Holy Spirit into you, and the Holy Spirit is a mighty Spirit. He is a Spirit of power. How can I live in this world? The world, the flesh, the devil, they remain the same. 'What is the point of believing your gospel?' says someone. 'I have got to go back into the same world, and all the forces of evil and of hell are still there against me, and I am still the same person.' No, you are not. Believe on the Lord Jesus Christ, and you become a new person, no longer under law, but under grace, no longer in Adam, but in Christ. And more, the Spirit of God is put into you, and he is a mighty Spirit. 'Work out your own salvation with fear and trembling,' says this Apostle to the Philippians, 'for it is God which worketh in you both to will and to do of his good pleasure' (2:12–13).

But also—and this to me is in many ways the most wonderful thing of all—the moment I become a child of God, the moment I realize that I am not in Adam but in Christ, the moment I come from being under the law to being under grace, do you know what it does for me? It opens the door of heaven to me and I can begin to pray.

And we have all known have we not, what it is to turn to God in prayer? Some of us remember during the last war, and during the 1914–18 war, reading of the terrible experiences of men torpedoed at sea. There they might be, in their little dinghies, for days on end. The food had ended, so had the water, and they were just drifting, and it seemed that everything had finished and there was nobody in sight to save them. They were frantic and did not know what to do. Then somebody would say, 'What about prayer?' None of them had prayed for years, or had ever thought about God, but in their trouble they remembered him. Exactly like the people on the *Titanic*, the unsinkable ship, sailing across the Atlantic in April 1912. On the Sunday afternoon, with the band playing and everybody enjoying themselves, delighting in this wonderful achievement of man in making a ship that could not sink—suddenly the thud. They had struck an iceberg, and the moment they struck the iceberg, the orchestra which had been playing dance music and jazz, began to play 'Nearer my God to thee, Nearer to thee'. We have all known what it is to turn to God in prayer, but the vital question is this: Can we pray? Have we any right to pray? What is prayer? Now prayer means entering into the presence of God. It means addressing that almighty holy God who is in heaven while we are on earth, the God we have ignored and spurned, and reviled and rejected. How can we go into his presence? The answer is that we cannot go into his presence as we are.

'God heareth not sinners' (Jn 9:31). There is only one way whereby a man can pray with any confidence and assurance, and it is in believing in the cross of our Lord Jesus Christ. Listen to the Apostle: 'Therefore being justified by faith, we have peace with God through our Lord Jesus Christ: by whom also we have access by faith into this grace wherein we stand . . . .' But he is fond of saying this, we find it everywhere. 'For through him,' says Paul to the Ephesians—by Christ—'we both have access by one Spirit unto the Father' (2:18). You cannot go to God except through Jesus Christ. He said it himself: 'I am the way, the truth, and the life: no man cometh unto the Father, but by me' (Jn 14:6). You may address 'whatever Gods may be', you may shout out in the dark hoping that some god will hear you. That is not prayer. Prayer means speaking to God who is in heaven, who is all powerful to bless. How can you do that? There is only one way.

Read again the author of the epistle to the Hebrews putting it in his own incomparable manner: 'Seeing then that we have a great high priest, that is passed into the heavens, Jesus the Son of God, let us hold fast our profession. For we have not an high priest which cannot be touched with the feeling of our infirmities; but was in all points tempted like as we are, yet without sin. Let us therefore come boldly unto the throne of grace, that we may obtain mercy, and find grace to help in time of need' (Heb 4:14–16). That is the problem. What do I do when I need help? What do I do when I am failing, when I am in an agony, in a crisis? I want grace to help in time of need. How can I get it? What right have I to speak to God? And there is only one answer. My only right to speak to God is that Christ has borne my punishment and has reconciled me to God, and has made me at peace with God or, as it is put in Hebrews 10:19–22, 'Having therefore, brethren, boldness to enter into the holiest, by the blood of Jesus, by a new and living way, which he hath consecrated for us, through the veil, that is to say, his flesh; and having an high priest over the house of God; let us draw near with a true heart, in full assurance of faith, having our hearts sprinkled from an evil conscience, and our bodies washed with pure water.' He opens the gate of heaven, and enables me to pray.

And he answers my every accuser. If you go down on your knees and try to pray to God and talk to the Almighty God, your accuser will begin to speak. You will be reminded of the holiness of God, and how do you answer? There is only one answer. It was satisfied on the cross. The law of God was answered and satisfied on the cross. Your conscience will speak, it will rake up old things. Your memory will be activated, and you will be feeling that you are hopeless and terrible. Your accuser is accusing you. How do you deal with it? There is only one way of dealing with it, and we find it expressed in one of our hymns:

> Be thou my shield and hiding-place,
> That, sheltered near Thy side,
> I may my fierce accuser face,
> And tell him thou hast died.

J. Newton

And he cannot answer. The blood of Jesus Christ, God's Son, cleanses us from all sin and unrighteousness.

And then, when your sense of uncleanness and unworthiness before that holy God makes you ashamed, what do you do? You can but offer this prayer:

> Oh lamb of God still keep me
> Close to thy wounded side,

—'Tis only there in safety
And peace I can abide.
What foes and snares surround me,
What lusts and fears within!
The grace that sought and found me
Alone can keep me clean.

James George Deck

Eternal Light! Eternal Light!
    How pure the soul must be,
When, placed within Thy searching sight,
It shrinks not, but with calm delight,
    Can live, and look on Thee!

The spirits that surround Thy throne
    May bear Thy burning bliss;
But that is surely theirs alone,
Since they have never, never known
    A fallen world like this.

O! how shall I, whose native sphere
    Is dark, whose mind is dim,
Before the Ineffable appear,
And on my naked spirit bear
    The uncreated beam?

How can I? There is only one answer:

There is a way for man to rise,
    To that sublime abode:
An offering and a sacrifice,
A Holy Spirit's energies,
    An Advocate with God—

These, these prepare us for the sight
    Of holiness above:
The sons of ignorance and night

May dwell [and shall dwell] in the Eternal Light,
Through [and only through] the Eternal Love!

T. Binney

'God forbid that I should glory, save in the cross of our Lord Jesus Christ.' He has given me that peace with God. He has given me a new nature. I am in Christ, I am no longer under the law, I am under grace, and he enables me to live. I can pray to God, I can answer my every enemy. I have a right to speak, even to the God of heaven, in all the glory of his holiness. So I say, and are you also not ready to say, 'God forbid that I should glory, save in the cross of our Lord Jesus Christ'?

Chapter 9

Bought Out and Set Free

Come, Thou Fount of every blessing,
  Tune my heart to sing Thy grace:
Streams of mercy, never ceasing,
  Call for songs of loudest praise.
Teach me some melodious measure,
  Sung by flaming tongues above:
O the vast, the boundless treasure
  Of my Lord's unchanging love!

R. Robinson

That is what we have been trying to do in our consideration of Paul's great words in Galatians—to take in the greatness of this boundless treasure. It is so grand, so glorious, that all efforts and endeavours will inevitably fail, and yet it is our business to look at it and to examine it and survey it, that something of the vastness of its glory may shine in upon us.

We must remember that the cross had been a stumbling block to Paul once. The idea that a saviour should die in helplessness upon a cross was ridiculous. The Saviour was to be a great and mighty man, a military person, a man of power who should be attended with great pomp and ceremony. The idea that this man who was born in a stable in Bethlehem and had worked as a carpenter, who had not even been trained as a Pharisee, the idea that he should be the long expected Messiah, and that this death of his upon the cross was the crowning glory of his life and of his coming, the thing was a stumbling block to him. It was ridiculous. It was blasphemy. Also, Paul had persecuted the church of Christ, and, as he told the very august company one day when he was appearing before the Roman governor Festus and King Agrippa, 'I verily thought with myself, that I ought to do many things contrary to the name of Jesus of Nazareth' (Acts 26:9). That was his position.

And the thing he especially despised was this death upon the cross. But yet, what he is saying here now is that this means everything to him. 'God forbid that I should glory, save in the cross of our Lord Jesus Christ, by whom the world is crucified unto me and I unto the world.' What he is saying here, is that this is the lynch pin, the centre of everything. This is the greatest thing in the world, the greatest thing that mankind has ever known, the greatest thing that ever happened. Notice that he does not say that he admires it, he does not say that he is going to try to set out to imitate it. Many have said both these things. He does not say that it is just one incident in a remarkable life, a tragic one, a very regrettable one, that is not what he says at all. Neither, let us observe, does he say that it is just something at the beginning of the Christian life. There are many Christians who have said that in one way or another. You start with the cross, they say, then you go on to what they call a deeper Christian life. The cross, they say, is only for conversion, the cross only deals with forgiveness of sins. It is something that marks the beginning, and then you go on and you do not come back any more to the cross. You start there, but then you leave it, and you go on to the deeper depths of the spiritual life.

That is not what the apostle Paul says. Here is a man

writing at the full height of his maturity as a Christian, the great apostle to the gentiles. At the very height of his experience he says, 'God forbid that I should glory, save in the cross of the Lord Jesus Christ.' He has not left it to go on to some higher reaches. The cross is still everything to him. Why? Because, he has found that everything proceeds from the cross. It is the source and the fount of everything that he has as a Christian, everything that he has become, everything that he can ever hope for. And what I have been trying to do is to draw out these different aspects of the cross which the great Apostle had come to see and which in his various epistles he helps us to see likewise. So now, let us look at it like this. We have seen that Paul says that the cross has put him in an entirely new position, that he was crucified with Christ, that when Christ died he died, and that that is true of all who believe in Christ, that they die with him, and they finish with the law, they are under grace, and they start living a new kind of life.

Now I want to consider that aspect of the matter a little further just to show again how everything proceeds from the cross, and how a Christian is a man who glories in the cross. If the cross is not central to you, you are not a Christian. You may say that you admire Jesus and his teaching, that does not make you a Christian. You can do that and be a Mohammedan. You can do that and still remain in the Jewish religion. You can do that and remain just a moralist. No, the cross is vital, the cross is central, everything comes out of it. Let me put it to you like this. The Apostle tells us that the cross governs his view of himself and that he has a new view of himself as a result of the cross. This, of course, has been implicit on several occasions already as we have seen as we have dealt with this matter, but I am now going to put it explicitly to you. I am going to work it out with you, because it is, after all, one of the most glorious aspects of this great doctrine of the cross of Christ. It gives a man an entirely different view of himself.

Now, how does that happen? If you read 2 Corinthians 5 you will find that he there expands this aspect in a particularly clear manner. He has got two great things to say: 'Wherefore,' he says in verse 16, 'henceforth know we no man after the flesh: yea, though we have known Christ after the flesh, yet now henceforth know we him no more.' That is one. But here is another in verses 14–15: 'For the love of Christ constraineth us; because we thus judge, that if one died for all, then were all dead: and that he died for all, that they which live should not henceforth live unto themselves, but unto him which died for them, and rose again.' What he is saying in that chapter is all summarized in verse 17 when he puts this astonishing statement before us: 'Therefore if any man be in Christ, he is a new creature, old things are passed away; behold, all things are become new.' And among the 'all things' that have become new, is a man's view of himself. He has an entirely new view of himself, and one of the most wonderful things that the cross of Christ does to a man who knows its meaning and understands what happened there, is that it delivers him from himself; and this is one of the most glorious deliverances a man can ever know, to be free and delivered from himself.

Let us work this out. The Apostle puts it like this. He says that a man as he is by nature, a man who is not a Christian and who has not seen the message of the cross, he has got a view of himself. And, according to the Apostle, he views himself after or, if you like, according to the flesh. Now if you are familiar with Paul's writings, you will know that he always makes a contrast between the flesh and the spirit. Seeing things 'after the flesh' means seeing things as they are without the light that the Lord Jesus Christ casts upon them through the Holy Spirit. So left to himself, without the light

of Christ, this is how man thinks of himself. He thinks of
himself always, of course, in terms of the things that are true
of him. Birth, this state into which he was born, where he
was born, his father and mother, grandfather, grandmother,
antecedents, lineage, all that concerns him, is all there. The
Apostle was never tired of referring to this, because of this
tremendous change that had taken place in him. He could
not get over it. Let me quote to you again what he says in
Philippians 3: 'Though I might also have confidence in the
flesh. If any other man thinketh he hath whereof he might
trust in the flesh, I more: circumcised the eighth day, of the
stock of Israel, of the tribe of Benjamin, an Hebrew of the
Hebrews; as touching the law, a Pharisee; concerning zeal,
persecuting the church; touching the righteousness which
is in the law, blameless' (vv. 5–6). That was how he used to
think about himself, and that is the sort of way in which
every man by nature thinks of himself. Birth, antecedents,
pedigree.

Not only that, he thinks in terms of his station in life, and
his position in life. What class are you born into? What is
your position? Then in terms of wealth. Born wealthy, born
poor. These are the distinctions, the world is full of them,
the world is divided up along these lines today, and we
know all about it, and we know of all the jealousy and the
rivalry, and we know of all the despising. It is there, this is
humanity, this is life, this is man without Christ. And then,
of course, he thinks of himself in terms of his inbred natural
powers and propensities. Has he got a good mind, or a good
brain? Can he think, or is he like those lesser breeds without
the law? Is he a man of understanding, or is he just a man
who is taken in by everything that comes along, and who
lives only for pleasure? A man thinks of himself in terms of
his ability, his knowledge, his understanding, his grasp of
affairs or of some particular study. These are the ways in

which a man thinks of himself.

And then he thinks in terms of his goodness. I am trying to reduce what the Apostle says about himself in Philippians 3 to a number of principles, to show that they are universally true. This is where you get the rivalry between nations, nationalism, and all the bitterness and the things that are destroying the modern world—apartheid, and anti-semitism and all the other things that are disgracing the life of humanity. All these arise because men think of themselves in natural human terms. And then other things come in—goodness, as against badness, and here religion comes in. People are proud of being religious, proud of the fact that they are religious, always brought up to be so, they say, carrying on a noble tradition. And these are the ways in which they tend to think of themselves. They do so entirely in terms of the way in which they find themselves, because a man does not determine his birth or who his parents are going to be; he does not choose his own pedigree, he does not choose his own powers, even. It does not behove us to be proud of any power we may have, we have not produced it. Shakespeare did not produce his powers, he was born with them. Every man is born in the way that he finds himself. We can use and develop the powers, but we cannot create them. That is where all this pride in these things is so monstrous and so ridiculous. So that is the first thing that the Apostle tells us about this view of self, without the light cast upon it by the cross of Christ.

The second characteristic of that view is that it is entirely self-centred. The Apostle puts it like this, when he says that '[He the Lord] died for all, that they which live should not henceforth live unto themselves, but unto him which died for them, and rose again' (2 Cor 5:15). Man by nature lives unto himself. Paul did. He did it as Saul of Tarsus; we have all done it. And this is one of the tragedies of man. Man lives for self in all its varied forms. Self-consciousness, awareness of self the whole time, watching self, regarding self, leading to pride in self. This, with the previous things, leads to pride, self conceit.

But perhaps the most troublesome thing of all and the most tragic thing of all is self-centredness, and this is the curse of the human race since men fell. What most of us need above everything else is to get away from ourselves, to forget ourselves. But we revolve around ourselves. We are the centre of our universe and we are always looking at ourselves, and everything is judged and evaluated in terms of us—what it means to me, what it does to me. All our rivalries, all our bitterness and jealousies come out of that. It is true of individuals, it is true of nations. Self-centredness. And then in addition to that, selfishness, of course. Wanting everything for this self. No wonder Paul says we should no longer live unto ourselves but unto him who died for us and rose again. The self-centred man or woman is always selfish, obviously. Feeding this self, pandering to it, wanting it to obtain things, wanting others not to have it, everything to build up and to satisfy this horrid, terrible self, which governs us and which controls us. All that leads, of course, to being sensitive, seeing insults where they are not meant, and where indeed they very often do not exist. Hyper-sensitive. Always afraid somebody is going to detract from us. Feeling somebody is trying to do so. Feeling hurt, feeling wounded. And that in turn leads to self-protection. Self-protectiveness. We spend a lot of our time protecting ourselves, even trying to avoid the possibility of something that might harm us. It becomes quite a great business, always protecting this delicate, hypersensitive self at the centre.

On top of all this, and this is the most mysterious thing of all about mankind, in spite of all I have just been saying, man as he is by nature is, in the main, self-reliant and self-confident. In other words, he believes that he has it in him to make a success. 'I am the master of my fate, I am the captain of my soul.' He does not like religion because it tells him that he cannot save himself. He objects to it. He believes that he can. He has the power, it is in him. 'Believe in thyself,' says the whole psychology of the world, and he is ready to do so. Trust yourself. Be yourself. So the life of man is governed in this way, by this entirely wrong and false view of himself. He lives through himself. He is the beginning and the end. He is his own god, he is autonomous. Self-centred, autonomous, modern independent man, who does not believe in a god because he does not need him, because he himself is someone, and yet you see that the whole time here he is, nervous, apprehensive, afraid, sensitive, hyper-sensitive. That is how this great man was as Saul of Tarsus, before he met the Son of God on the road to Damascus, and saw the meaning of his death upon the cross.

What difference, then, did it make? Well, let me give a new view. 'If any man be in Christ he is a new creature: old things are passed away'—all that has gone—'behold all things are become new' (2 Cor 5:17). And there was nothing that thrilled this mighty man more than the new view that he now had of himself. He had been liberated from all that old life. It was a terrible life when he really saw what it meant. It was a sham, it was a fraud; it was always insecure and it never gave real peace of heart, rest and satisfaction. But now it is all different. He has a new view of himself through the cross. It is the cross that has really shown himself to himself. He has seen that he, like everybody else, is a sinner, and a vile sinner at that. He has seen that he is full of sin, that he is unworthy, that he is vile. Once a man sees himself in the light of the cross, he sees the horror of that self-centred view in its every aspect. It is all wrong; it is not true. It is because that view is not true of any of us, that the world is as it is, with all the strife and tension and the animosity, the unhappiness and the misery. Self is the cause of all these things.

So here you find that the Apostle when he comes to write about himself and about men in general, now begins to say things like this—'There is none righteous, no, not one' (Rom 3:10). You see, he had said before that touching the righteousness which is of the law he was blameless, but that was because he had got his own private interpretation of the law, as all the Pharisees had. Now he sees the truth of the law, and he is convicted. The law says 'Thou shalt not covet,' and the moment a man realizes that coveting is a sin, he knows he is a sinner. Everybody has sinned. You may not have done the thing, but if you wanted to, and if, perhaps, the only reason why you did not do it was because you had not the courage to do it, that means you are a terrible sinner. Coveting, condemned, the law revived, sin revived, I died.

He says the whole world lieth guilty before God. 'There is none righteous, no, not one.' 'For all have sinned, and come short of the glory of God,' and he is involved, he is among them. And not only that, he sees that he is a failure. This man who had been so self-confident and self-satisfied, so proud of his morality and his religion, and his knowledge of the law, cries out in an agony, 'Oh wretched man that I am! who shall deliver me from the body of this death?' (Rom 7:24). Sin within him, sin in his members. He knows what he wants to do but he cannot do it. He knows the law is good and righteous and holy, but he himself is sold under sin. To do good, he says, is one thing, to desire to do good is one thing, to do it is another thing. When I would do good, evil is present with me, 'For the good that I would I do not: but the evil which I would not, that I do' (Rom 7:19). Here I am—with my mind I desire to keep the law of God, but I find another law in my members, dragging me down and enslaving me.

He had seen all that, so now he has an entirely new view of himself, and he realizes that he is entirely without strength. He commends the love of God in Christ to the Romans by putting it like this, 'For when we were yet without strength, in due time Christ died for the ungodly.' We were without strength. 'But God commendeth his love toward us, in that while we were yet sinners, Christ died for us' (5:6, 8). And again, 'For if, when we were enemies, we were reconciled to God ...' (v.10). But he thought he was serving God. He thought he was a most godly man, and very pleasing in God's sight. He says—I came to see that I was an enemy of God, I was not worshipping and serving God, I was worshipping and serving myself. That is why I was proud of my morality, proud of my religion, proud of my understanding. I was not serving God, I was my god, though I thought I was pleasing God.

It is the cross that showed him all this, because, there on the cross, what the Lord Jesus Christ was telling him, telling all of us, was that he had come into this world, and had had to go to the death on the cross, because we are what we are: because we are sinners, because we are failures, because we are helpless, because we are lost, that there is no good thing in us, more, that we are dead, spiritually dead, and to be spiritually dead means that we do not know God. We may talk about God, but we do not know him. That is what spiritual death means. Our Lord says, 'And this is life eternal, that they might know thee the only true God, and Jesus Christ, whom thou hast sent' (Jn 17:3), and to be dead is the exact opposite. It means that you do not know God, that you do not know Jesus Christ.

Now, God is a living God, and he wants to be known. He made man in order that man might know him and in order that he might have fellowship with him. Man was meant to be the companion of God, and you and I are not merely to

discuss God or to talk about God as if he were some philosophic x. God is to be known, the God who spoke to
Abraham as a friend. Abraham knew him and so did Isaac
and Jacob. All these men, the patriarchs and the saints of the
Old Testament, they knew God. David speaks to him with an
intimacy. Do you know God? If you do not, it is because you
are dead, spiritually dead, and the Apostle came to see that
that was his state and condition. 'And you hath he quickened,'
he says to the Ephesians, 'who were dead in trespasses and
sins' (Eph 2:1) and he was one of them. 'The children of
wrath,' he says, 'even as others' (Eph 2:3). At the cross Paul
comes to see all this. The cross shows him that the Son of
God would never have died on that cross but for the fact
that men were in this desperate plight. If they could have
been saved in any other way, they would have been. But it
was not possible, and therefore the cross proclaims that man
is completely hopeless and vile. But thank God, it does not
stop there. You see, what Paul had learned from the cross is
that the Lord Jesus Christ had died for him there in order to
deliver him.

Now many terms are used to explain this, and one of them
is the term of paying a ransom, paying a price. Man has
become the slave of the devil and of sin, and of evil, and he
has got to be bought. The Apostle says that he discovered
that what was happening on the cross, was that the Lord
Jesus Christ was purchasing him, so he writes to the Corinthians about morality and behaviour and he puts it like this:
'What?' he says, 'know ye not that your body is the temple of
the Holy Ghost which is in you, which ye have of God, and
ye are not your own? For ye are bought with a price: therefore glorify God in your body, and in your spirit, which are
God's' (1 Cor 6:19–20).

Now then, here the new view comes in. He was the slave
of the devil, the slave of the world, the slave of sin, and of

evil. He could not get free, try as he would. But he has been
bought out. He has been delivered, he has been set free. He
has been translated from the kingdom of darkness into the
kingdom of God's Son. He has been redeemed. And now he
has got a new view of himself. He is not his own, he does not
belong to himself any more. He formerly lived to himself,
but no longer, he has been bought with a price. He has a
new life, he is in a new world. You know, this so grips and
thrills this man, that he cannot stop saying it. He says it
everywhere. I have quoted you 1 Corinthians 6:19–20, but
listen to him saying it in Galatians 2:20, the very epistle we
are studying: 'I,' he says, 'am crucified with Christ: nevertheless I live; yet not I, but Christ liveth in me: and the life
which I now live in the flesh I live by the faith of the Son of
God who loved me, and gave himself for me.' You see the
difference, what a tremendous statement this is: 'I live, yet
not I.' In other words, he says, I am not what I was. I used to
live to myself, and for myself. Now I live, yet not I. It is not
that any longer, it is this: 'I live; yet not I, but Christ liveth in
me: and the life which I now live in the flesh I live by the
faith of the Son of God, who loved me, and gave himself for
me'—on the cross.

So you see, it is an entirely new type of life. He is not
living as he was before. The cross has changed everything
for him. He lives now not unto himself—'I live by the faith of
the Son of God, who loved me, and gave himself for me.' Or
listen to him saying it again, in the epistle to the Romans at
the beginning of chapter 8. 'There is therefore now no condemnation to them which are in Christ Jesus, who walk not
after the flesh, but after the Spirit. For'—note this—'the law
of the Spirit of life in Christ Jesus hath made me free from
the law of sin and death.' He used to live the life of the law,
unto the law of sin and death, a life of sinning and condemnation and fear of death and the grave, of bondage, of

the tyranny of that life under the law. 'The law of the Spirit of life in Christ Jesus hath made me free . . .' he is no longer living there, he is living here, he is a new man. He has an entirely new outlook upon life and it is all summed up in that great phrase, 'I, yet not I, but Christ liveth in me'. He is no longer living unto or for himself, but he is living unto him who died for him and rose again. That is his great argument in 2 Corinthians 5, '. . . because we thus judge,' he says, 'that if one died for all, then were all dead: and that he died for all, that they which live should not henceforth live unto themselves, but unto him which died for them, and rose again.' It is an absolutely new life with an entirely new view of himself, what he is, what he is meant to be: 'old things are passed away; behold, all things are become new.' I, yet not I. 'I live by the faith of the Son of God, who loved me, and gave himself for me.'

Is it surprising that this man glories in the cross? He is still living in this world, and people can be very difficult, so he writes like this in the first epistle to the Corinthians: 'Let a man so account of us, as of the ministers of Christ, and stewards of the mysteries of God' (4:1). When you think of me, he says, think of me like that. Do not think of me as Paul, because the moment you do that you will think of Apollos and Cephas and you will be arguing which is the greater man. Think of us as the steward ministers of Christ and stewards of the mysteries of God. 'Moreover,' he says, 'it is required in stewards, that a man be found faithful.' And further: 'But with me, it is a very small thing that I should be judged of you, or of man's judgment: yea, I judge not mine own self. For I know nothing by myself; yet am I not hereby justified: but he that judgeth me is the Lord' (1 Cor 4:2–4). What a deliverance. Look, says Paul, you really do not trouble me. Say what you like about me, you cannot affect me any longer. With me, it is a very small thing that I be judged of you or of any man's judgement. Do you know that experience? Are you like that? Are you immune to criticism? Can you say that you are unconcerned by what people think about you? Can you not see that it would be heaven to be able to say that? Think of the misery and the unhappiness that is caused to you because you are afraid of what people think, what people say. Here is a man who has been delivered from himself, and says, 'with me it is a very small thing that I should be judged of you, or of any man's judgment: yea, I judge not mine own self.' Not only does he not worry about what other people think of him, he has even stopped thinking about himself.

Have you ever thought of the amount of time you waste in thinking about yourself—looking at yourself, preening yourself, examining yourself, awarding marks, afraid of others? A sheer waste of time, and an abomination. I am not only not concerned, he says, about what other people think of me, I do not even think about myself. I have finished with myself, my judge is the Lord, and I live to him and to his praise, I, yet not I. 'I live by the faith of the Son of God, who loved me, and who gave himself for me.' What a change. What a deliverance. And it is the cross that has done it all. You are not your own, because you have been bought with a price, and the price was the precious blood of Christ, 'as of a lamb without blemish and without spot'.

Now, because of this new view of himself, Paul has also got an entirely new view of the whole of life and all its attendant circumstances. He now knows how to live in a new way, and we all need to learn that, do we not? Before, it was a question of moral striving, vain effort, trying to be good, trying to keep the law, trying to be moral, trying to be religious. But having to do it all himself. And all being done for self and all leading to nothing but utter, absolute, failure. And another of the wonderful things that is done to us by the cross of Christ, when we truly understand its meaning, is that it changes all that. It enables us to live in an entirely new manner. Read again what this same man, the apostle Paul, writes to the Romans. Look at chapter 8 again. I have already quoted verses 1 and 2, and I will now quote verses 3 and 4: 'For what the law could not do, in that it was weak through the flesh, God sending his own Son in the likeness of sinful flesh, and for sin, condemned sin in the flesh: that the righteousness of the law might be fulfilled in us, who walk not after the flesh, but after the Spirit.' It is the whole explanation of the cross. It was on the cross that God condemned sin and the flesh in order that the righteousness of the law might be fulfilled in us who walk not after the flesh but after the Spirit. In other words, the cross gives a man an entirely new outlook upon how to live life in this world.

And this is how it does it. Before a man sees the meaning of the message of the cross, he thinks in terms of good and bad, he thinks in terms of actions, but he cannot get any further, and because he cannot get any further, he cannot do what he wants to do. But the cross gives us an entirely new view of sin, and it shows us that sin is our greatest enemy. It shows us things we like and things we are fond of, and things the world dazzles before us, as the enemies of our souls. They are the things that put us in jeopardy. It shows us that what the world glories in is what has brought us to our present misery. It is the thing that makes us unhappy, it is the thing that produces all the problems. The thing that seemed so wonderful is the thing that makes us afraid to die and afraid of God—that is what it really is. The cross strips it of all its gaudy colouring and reveals it unto us in its vileness and foulness.

And it does it in this way. What was it that brought the Son of God to the cross? The answer is sin. Sin. Rebellion against God. This principle of evil. The selfishness of man.

This is the thing that crucified him. Man sees it for what it is for the first time. Not only that, it gives him another revelation, and I will explain it like this. Sin is that which contradicts the whole purpose of God in Christ and the whole purpose of the Son of God in going to the cross and dying in that cruel and shameful manner. Paul puts it to Titus in these glowing words: he says, 'For the grace of God that bringeth salvation hath appeared to all men, teaching us that, denying ungodliness and worldly lusts, we should live soberly, righteously, and godly, in this present world; looking for that blessed hope, and the glorious appearing of the great God and our Saviour Jesus Christ; who gave himself for us ...'. What for? To save us from hell? Read on, 'that he might redeem us from all iniquity, and purify unto himself a peculiar people, zealous of good works' (2:11–14). He gave himself for us on the cross in order that he might deliver us from that evil life. He did it to prepare for himself a special people, a possession for himself, a people zealous of good works, to 'redeem us from all iniquity'. So if I go on living that self-centred life, I am denying the very thing that took him to the cross. Not only that, I am denying everything I claim to believe as a Christian.

A man who has seen the message of the cross, and yet goes on sinning, is a man who is contradicting himself. 'What shall we say then? Shall we continue in sin, that grace may abound? God forbid. How shall we, that are dead [or that die] to sin, live any longer therein?' (Rom 6:1–2). Listen, says Paul, if you go on sinning you are denying all you believe. And again, 'Likewise reckon ye also yourselves to be dead indeed unto sin, but alive unto God through Jesus Christ our Lord. Let not sin therefore reign in your mortal body, that ye should obey it in the lusts thereof. Neither yield ye your members as instruments of unrighteousness unto sin: but yield yourselves unto God, as those that are alive from the dead, and your members as instruments of righteousness unto God' (Rom 6:11–13). That means, you see, just this: that your sanctification is governed by your view of the cross. You do not say that the cross is only about justification, or the cross is only about conversion and that then we leave that and we go to the higher reaches, and are in the realm of the Holy Spirit only. No. The cross governs sanctification. It is the mightiest argument for sanctification. You are contradicting your own initial beliefs if you continue in sin and are not living the holy life, or, in the words of the apostle John, 'Beloved, now are we the sons of God, and it doth not yet appear what we shall be: but we know that, when he shall appear, we shall be like him; for we shall see him as he is. And every man that hath this hope in him purifieth himself, even as he is pure' (1 Jn 3:2–3).

Once a man sees the message of the cross, he has an entirely new view of everything. He is not just trying to live a good life now; not just trying not to do harm; not trying to live just on the edge of the law—not wanting to be prosecuted, but going as far as he safely can. That is all finished. He is a new man. He has been bought with a price, he is a son of God. He is being prepared for him. He has a new motive. To sin now means that he is wounding love, he is not breaking a law. He is wounding the love of the one who gave himself for him. He says, I cannot do it. I have been bought with a price. I have no right to do it, I am not my own. I belong to him. I am a slave of Christ as I used to be the slave of the devil and of sin. I have no right to, and I cannot do it. He has a new conception of sin, he has new motives for living a holy life, and thank God, over and above all, he has got new power whereby to do it.

For the Christ of God died not only that we might be forgiven but that we might receive the gift of the Holy Spirit and his power. He teaches us how to live, and he also teaches us how to suffer. Because we live in a world of suffering and we need to be taught how to suffer, he teaches us how to suffer. The cross teaches us how to suffer, not only how to live morally and ethically, but how to suffer, 'The slings and arrows of outrageous fortune'. They come to us all: misunderstanding, people misunderstanding us, injustices done to us, the failure of trusted friends, people in whom we reposed every confidence letting us down, disappointments, loneliness, physical pain. How do you stand up to these things? These are the things that come to all of us, how do we meet them, how do we live? This is the way: read what the apostle Peter says about this. 'Servants, be subject to [obey] your masters with all fear; not only to the good and gentle, but also to the froward. For this is thankworthy, if a man for conscience toward God endure grief, suffering wrongfully. For what glory is it, if, when ye be buffeted for your faults, ye shall take it patiently? but if, when ye do well, and suffer for it, ye take it patiently, this is acceptable with God. For even hereunto were ye called: because Christ also suffered for us, leaving us an example, that ye should follow his steps: who did no sin, neither was guile found in his mouth: who, when he was reviled, reviled not again; when he suffered, he threatened not: but committed himself to him that judgeth righteously: who his own self bear our sins in his own body on the tree, that we, being dead to sins, should live unto righteousness: by whose stripes ye were healed. For ye were as sheep going astray, but are now returned unto the Shepherd and Bishop of your souls' (1 Pet 2:18–25). There is the only way, the cross—misunderstanding, injustice, treachery of friends, the loneliness, even his disciples forsaking him and fleeing from him. In the dark night, they all forsook him and fled, and left him alone. But he had known that it was coming, he had told them that when he said: 'The hour cometh ... that ye shall be scattered ... and shall leave me alone: and yet,' he says, and yet, 'I am not alone, because the Father is with me' (Jn 16:32).

And so it is, that no experience can ever fall to your lot but that he has gone through it. The treachery, the misunderstanding, the abuse, the injustice, the loneliness, the agony, the sweat:

> In every pang that rends the heart,
> The Man of Sorrows had a part.
>
> *M. Bruce*

Yes, in the light of the fact that he has been made in the likeness of sinful flesh, and 'was in all points tempted like as we are, yet without sin', he is able to succour us.

So the cross not only teaches me how to live, it teaches me how to suffer, how I should follow in his steps. And it also teaches me how to die, that we have all got to die. And it is only the cross that really can teach me how to die. Let me show you some of the ways in which it does that. He has taken the sting out of death. You see death is not the trouble, it is what follows death that is the trouble. Men say nothing happens after death, but they do not know, and they cannot prove it, and they do not really believe it. The last enemy is the fear of death, who is ever waiting for us with that scythe of his. Ah, but it is all right. Hear this great Apostle as he puts it again to the Corinthians. Oh this corruptible, he says, must put on incorruption and this mortal must put on immortality. 'So when this corruptible shall have put on incorruption, and this mortal shall have put on immortality, then shall be brought to pass the saying that is written, Death is swallowed up in victory. O death, where is thy sting? O grave, where is thy victory? The sting of death is sin; and the strength of sin is the law. But thanks be to God, which giveth us the victory through our Lord Jesus Christ' (1 Cor 15:54–

57). By dying on the cross he satisfied the law and he has taken the sting out of death to all who believe in him and in the efficacy of his atoning sacrificial death. He has taken the sting out of it. He has conquered death and the grave, but in addition to this, by dying there upon the cross he has shown us how to die.

Do you remember how the author of the epistle to the Hebrews puts it? 'Wherefore seeing we also are compassed about with so great a cloud of witnesses, let us lay aside every weight, and the sin which doth so easily beset us, and let us run with patience the race that is set before us, looking unto Jesus, the author and finisher of our faith; who for the joy that was set before him endured the cross, despising the shame . . .' and the cross was a terrible thing for him, that was why he had been sweating in the garden. He knew that when the sins of men were placed upon him he would lose the face of God and suffer in his righteous soul a death. The author of life dying, he did not want to. This was terrible, but he endured it. How? '. . . For the joy that was set before him, he endured the cross, despising the shame, and is set down at the right hand of the throne of God. For consider him that endured such contradiction of sinners against himself, lest ye be wearied and faint in your minds. Ye have not yet resisted unto blood, striving against sin' (Heb 12:1–4). But he did, and he teaches us how to die.

You have only to look at him dying on that cross to realize that the sting has gone. And that he has gone on as he said to prepare a place for you. 'Let not your heart be troubled,' he said, 'ye believe in God, believe also in me. In my Father's house are many mansions: if it were not so, I would have told you. I go to prepare a place for you. And if I go and prepare a place for you, I will come again, and receive you unto myself; that where I am, there ye may be also' (Jn 14:1–3). So look at this apostle Paul later in his life. He was a prisoner in Rome, his captor was none other than the notorious Emperor Nero, an unprincipled, unjust, capricious dictator, and the Apostle was hearing rumours almost every day as to when he was to be put to death. And he knew it was coming, and could come at any moment, but this is how he faced it: 'According to my earnest expectation and my hope, that in nothing I shall be ashamed, but that with all boldness, as always, so now also Christ shall be magnified in my body, whether it be by life, or by death. For to me to live is Christ, and to die is gain. But if I live in the flesh, this is the fruit of my labour: yet what I shall choose I wot not. For I am in a strait betwixt two, having a desire to depart, and to be with Christ; which is far better: nevertheless to abide in the flesh is more needful for you' (Phil 1:20–24). That is the way to face death. And now that death is gain, that death means to be with Christ, which is far better, death is no longer a spectre, not since the death of the Son of God. He saw the way to heaven, and to die, if you believe in him and his death, means to go to be with him. To be with Christ, which is far better. It is gain.

And so you see that out of this cross come all these wonderful things. Man is delivered from his petty self, he is taught how to live and enabled to live in that way. He is taught how to suffer whatever may come. He is taught how to die victoriously and triumphantly, because he knows that Christ by dying conquered death and his death led to the glory of the resurrection, the ascension, and his sitting in the glory at the right hand of God.

It is not surprising is it, that this man says, 'God forbid that I should glory, save in the cross of the Lord Jesus Christ'? What else is there? This is everything. Every good thing comes out of this. Without this there is nothing. With this there is everything—in this world, in life, in death, and in the glory everlasting, which awaits the children, the people of God.

Are you glorying in the cross of Christ? Or are you still glorying in yourself? Have you seen yourself? Look to the cross, and you will see yourself, you will hate yourself, and you will pray to be delivered and he will tell you that he has delivered you. He died that you might say, 'I live, yet not I, but Christ liveth in me: and the life which I now live in the flesh I live by the faith of the Son of God, who loved me, and gave himself for me.' I am not my own, I have been bought with a price. I belong to him, who loved me so well that he died for me, and ever liveth to make intercession for me, and who will come again and receive me unto himself.

> Oh the vast, the boundless treasure
> Of my Lord's unchanging love.

R. Robinson

Scripture Index